Introduction

This book gives a brief history of Attila and the Huns and their conquest of Central Europe (modern-day Hungary) and the destruction of Rome, which led to the eventual fall of the Roman Empire. The first thing you'll learn about the Huns is their history and where they came from, along with why Attila the Hun was one of the evilest people in history. You will then learn about Attila's conquest of Gneisses, Constantinople, and his conflict with the Visigoths.

Additionally, there is a section specifically devoted to the Battle of the Catalaunian Plains, which covers Attila's tactics. In this section, you will learn why these psychological and military strategies were so successful and are still employed today.

Next, you'll learn how Attila held Rome in terror by paying a man yearly not to conquer Rome, but you'll also learn how he devised a strategy and the ideal justification for an invasion of the Western Roman Empire. The reason Attila the Hun was also known as The Scourge of God or The Man Who Broke Rome will finally become clear to you. Last but not least, you will learn ten shocking facts about Attila and the Huns. If you're up for the adventure, let's start by figuring out why Attila was the most evenly matched guy in history.

Chapter *1*

The Most Evil Men in History

In the fifth century, one guy terrorized and destroyed millions of people in Europe. All who stopped in their way were subjected to torture, rape, and murder by Attila the Hun and his merciless barbarians.

They are said to have drunk women's blood, dipped their arrows in embryonic liquid, and were related to evil spirits. The brutality of Attila knew no bounds. He killed his brother and slew deserters. His merciless hunts frightened the powerful Roman Empire with their savagery. In their quest for gold, they leveled enormous cities and slaughtered entire populations.

He was thought by Christians to have been sent from Hell to punish sinners. Attila earned the moniker "scourge of god."

He was unique compared to everyone else. He was more effective than anyone else and more vicious than elsewhere. He gave everyone the willies. There were high expectations for Attila from the moment he was born in 406 AD. He would have grown up in a vast extended royal family knowing that he would have to struggle for power and that the stakes were quite high because if he lost, he would die.

Attila was terrified as a very young child despite his riches. One custom associated with the Huns is that newborn males had their cheeks cut off to teach them to endure pain at a young age. He was encouraged to ride before he could walk, like other Hunnic men. They almost were born in the saddle; they also dine, talk, and conduct diplomatic negotiations while mounted. Of course, the ancient sources who claim that if you take a ham off a horse, he can't walk, are exaggerating this. Attila's followers were despised for their brutal pillaging. They originated in Mongolia, moved west, and established themselves in Pannonia on the Danube where Budapest is now.

The powerful Roman Empire ruled across Europe in the fifth century. Their alliance with the brutal Huns was precarious. By the time the Huns are established on the vast Hungarian plain, they have already become somewhat parasitic on the Roman Empire in a different sense—they are taking money. They do this occasionally by paying annual tribute to the

Romans, and occasionally they do it by working as mercenaries for the Roman army.

Attila was raised in a brutally violent environment where only the strong were able to survive. His upbringing would have been rather unstable because the Huns were always at war with other tribes and there were also ongoing difficulties within the royal family. It is very debatable whether he is there to command or to be symbolic at that point, but he would likely have been given his group of warriors to lead at a very young age and probably in his mid-teens. His job at that point would have been to stand in the front and inspire courage in his warriors while also learning to face up to battle himself. Political power rewarded his courageous leadership.

Attila and his brother Bleda start to appear sometime between 435 and 440, and for a while, the two of them co-rule this Hunnic tribe. The power-hungry Attila was furious with this agreement, but Bleda had significant support, so he had to wait it out for the time being. Attila launched a string of violent invasions into the Roman territory between the ages of 20 and 30.

The barbarian stereotype, in particular the steppe nomad barbarians, is always a negative one. They are highly fearsome and dangerous militarily, and the entire society that appears with all of its warrior males on horseback is terrifying. The Huns had a reputation for using fatal lightning strikes. They can cover a lot of terrains, launch raids deep into vulnerable or only partially fortified provinces, and produce a dreadful shock wave of panic throughout Central Europe because you never knew when these people would show up at your door. Attila is connected to the Hunnic bow, which is the foundation of the Hunnic method of battle. They could kill a man at a range of 150 meters while mounted and fire arrows while standing.

The medieval version of the Blitzkrieg was a Hunnic tactic. The records mention that the Huns always pretended to flee at that point because they were able to wait outside the range of the majority of their foes, fill them with arrows, and make them brush at them. The Huns would then turn around and kill them one at a time once the adversaries had lost their coherence and cohesion. Along the Danube, Attila established a network of informants in addition to his devastating military prowess. There is a grapevine that operates along the frontier because most of his significant triumphs occur when the Romans are otherwise occupied.

For instance, he is aware that the main Danubian Army has been sent to Sicily to attempt to retake North Africa from the Vandals during his first significant campaign in 441. He is given the chance to attack by Nutz, and his successes go on to establish his reputation. He understood the worth of a formidable reputation. He scares people with his use of terror. Sacking cities is the best method to achieve this. A few years later, while a troop of Romans is traveling along, they are forced to stop short of the river because it is filled with the bones of the dead, having approached the city of noises on the Danube early on and forcing their way into the city and sacking the city.

Life was cheap for the cruel army of Attila. The rights of others were unimportant to the Huns. Numerous records purport to be statements made by Hunnic authorities about Romans or other people. It's rather typical for these nomads to divide the world into two categories: themselves and everyone else's slaves, who are completely disposable.

Therefore, in this world, you are either dominant or dominated, and if you are dominated, you are entirely disposable. They would cause the most deaths possible with no regard for human life at all, which is a trait of terrorists. Even though Attila had experienced victory outside, he was growing impatient with his brother at home and yearned for total control.

For many years, Attila and Bleda worked together as either joint leaders of the entire Hunna tribe or as heads of various Hunna factions. However, Attila was the type of man who had to govern by himself, thus in the end, it would either be him or Bleda. Attila killed his brother Bleda while he was sleeping. He took over as the only Hun leader at the age of 40. He wanted to strengthen the Hunnic military apparatus. He called together several tribes because he knew how potent a unified barbarian combat force would be against the Romans.

Consolidating the Coalition with the Ostrogoths, Gapids, and other subordinate tribes occupied his early years as king. He could then begin his career of terrifying cities once that was finished. After gaining governmental dominance over the Huns, the fervently superstitious Attila turned to religion for direction. Attila would have grown up hearing the Huns' legends about their purpose in life. Their achievement was a result of divine intervention.

Attila's captivating image included a crucial instance when a rusty old sword was recovered and brought to him as a sign from God. At this point, Attila declared that the gods' gift of the blade to him proved that he was meant to rule. Attila is ecstatic to learn that this is the sword of God, which ensures his victory, and he naturally informs everyone about it. He seeks fame, glory, and admiration, and while these things are a means to an end for him to get more power and wealth, they also end in themselves since every great leader seeks to honor glory and a good reputation. Attila was in charge of the allied barbarian tribes at this point, and he had the gods on his side. He was prepared to take on the Roman Empire, a superpower.

A half million vicious barbarian warriors were at the disposal of Attila, king of the Huns. He started undertaking raids for loot into the Eastern Roman Empire. His forces crossed the Black Sea and the Mediterranean in 446. They murdered civilians, ransacked churches, and desecrated sinners' graves. These post-apocalyptic images delighted Attila. He would smirk in satisfaction at the dread he caused. More than a hundred cities were subdued by him. No one was able to count the number of lives lost today. He didn't have a geographical purpose for this massacre, though.

The Huns' leadership depended on successful raiding operations. They would be subject to overthrow if they were unable to bring in wealth from outside sources. He also threatened the Romans with violence to demand payment. Attila was an effective war leader, able to compel the Romans to send up an increasing quantity of gold each year. We're discussing payments to Attila that are negotiated under treaties. Just to keep the Huns off the backs of the Romans and to keep the Huns happy as far as these treaties are concerned, 350 pounds of gold per year, which is doubled to 700, which is tripled to 2100 pounds of gold per year in a third treaty. This indicates that Attila is the conduit through which this gold enters these Hunnic groups' systems.

These accords were cleverly exploited by Attila to terrorize his people. Attila's requirement that deserters be given their money back was an act of brutality towards the disloyal. He frequently included this clause in his treaties with the Romans, and when the deserters are returned, they are not put back into the honey army; instead, they are put to death to deter the other soldiers. This rule made it clear that there was no use in deserting since, while you might manage to escape safely, Attila would pursue you, frighten the Romans, negotiate a deal to get your return, and then brutally murder you once he had you.

Due to Attila's polygamy, his women harbored intense resentment for one another. Gudrun, an unhappy spouse, persuaded him into eating both of his sons because she was so enraged with the tiller. His ugly character, which had already gained widespread acclaim, was greatly strengthened by this lie. Of course, all early Christian writers were horrified by the Huns. He is given several many names, such as flag Elam Dei or The Scourge of God. Before his picture switching between directions. It's a play on the Romans, and the Hun Empire operates a massive protection ring against the Roman government, extorting money and threatening violence.

At the same time, he must manage this multi-ethnic Empire, therefore part of Attila's charisma and ability to instill fear is meant to control various factions. While this was going on, his soldiers continued to assault the eastern Roman Empire. Attila rampaged over Greece and Eastern Europe, ruthlessly murdering Roman civilians, and only abated his horrific invasion in exchange for a sizable sum of cash from the Romans. He devastated and terrified people to such an extent that he had no opposition in the Eastern Roman Empire. Now that Attila could plan his assault on the West.

Attila was presented with an exceptional offer in 450 from an unexpected source. The Western Roman Emperor's sister, Anuria, was discovered to be having an affair with the household manager. The Imperial was very upset by this because it was a very scandalous thing for an emperor's sister to do, and he planned to marry her off to a nice, safe minor politician.

Anuria didn't like the concept; she wanted to be in charge of her destiny. She claimed to have gotten in touch with Attila and proposed to him, sending him her engagement ring as a sign of her sincerity. An imperial lady appeared to be proposing to him for marriage here. When this message reached the vast Hungarian plain, Attila would have laughed uncontrollably. Nothing about his actions after then suggests that he had any real ambition to go marry Anuria and rule the Western Empire; even Attila knew enough about European geography to know that she was living in Italy, not

Gaul, where he traveled next. When you get married, you anticipate the woman would bring a dowry with her. A sizable portion of the Western Roman Empire was requested by Attila as Anuria's dowry. He invaded the Roman Empire in the West to recoup his losses after his request was turned down.

Attila had the justification he required to invade Western Europe with the full force of his unified barbarian army. They wanted to cause widespread destruction. The Huns encountered St. Ursula, the eternal virgin while passing through Cologne. She was so stunning that Attila was enamored. He put his mission with her on hold and offered marriage. She declined, and an enraged Attila had her slaughtered along with 11,000 of her fellow pilgrims. He invades Northern Gaul; one of the first cities he reaches is Metz, which he totally ransacked and then massacred. Attila's troops arrived in Chalons by May 451.

At the Battle of Chalons, they ran against the superior Western Roman army here. The Huns were halted in their tracks for the first time. This was one of the most important wars in global history; had the Huns defeated the Romans, Europe may have been under barbarian rule, and modern Europeans might have possessed features similar to those of the Mongols in Asia. The Roman army defeats Attila's forces until they are forced to retreat. One minor detail that may or may not be accurate is that Attila's forces are pushed back and fighting from a barricade made of their saddles. As a result, their horses are being slaughtered in large numbers and they are engaged in fierce combat. The Hun fatalities were so great that rivers of blood flowed, forcing those who were thirsty from the battle to drink blood-tinted water.

The first image damage was caused by the Battle of Chalons, and reports said that there was a severe crisis of trust following the combat on the first day. Attila is shown in his camp preparing a large funeral pyre out of saddles on which he intends to burn himself to death before trusted advisors convince him that, in reality, things aren't quite as bad as they seem and there's no need to go to such absurd lengths. Nevertheless, this represents a setback.

The following year, Attila invades Northern Italy undeterred despite his reaction rousing fate elsewhere. The Roman Empire was shattered by Attila. fell city by city. Many were unwilling to fight him because of his fierce reputation. They opened the door to the barbarians and begged Attila to show them pity, but he refused. He had to regain his position over the Huns by achieving a string of spectacular victories to at least partially make up for the setback in Gaul. Attila's conquest of Italy, the center of the former Roman Empire, serves as evidence that the old magic is still at work. These

Italian cities are brimming with breathtaking beauty and priceless treasures.

Therefore, a suitably successful campaign in northern Italy can satisfy both the terror and the greed perspective on the two pillars on which the Hunnic Empire rests. Until his army was stationed at the gates of Rome, he frightened his way through northern Europe. A mission led by Pope Leo the First was despatched by the terrified Roman Emperor Valentinian to request a truce. This worked out well for Attila because his army was plagued by illness and slowed down by looting. He asked for gold and safe return home.

At that point, Attila was in a terrible position. To protect his central base, which was essential to his ability to function at all, he had to retreat backward to Pannonia if it were true that his army was sick and that the Eastern Roman Emperor was a threat to his base. Having received his reward, Attila was upset by the outbreak of peace. He brought plenty of Roman wealth back to Pannonia and made threats to launch another invasion as soon as he could. These predictions never came to pass because his reign of terror was about to come to an end.

At the age of 48, in the year 453 AD, he married Ildikó, a stunning German noblewoman. The Huns drank their usual amount of alcohol to celebrate the wedding. When they broke in, they discovered Attila dead and his young wife sobbing in the shadows of her veil. He had fallen to his back in a drunken stupor, suffered a nose hemorrhage, and the blood flowed back into his lungs and killed him. He was interred in a riverbed within three coffins made of iron, silver, and gold. Attila effectively never passed away since he was secretly interred, and those who did so were afterward assassinated so that no one would know where the cemetery was. Even though Attila the Hun only governed his people for eight years, the terror he inflicted on the inhabitants of fifth-century Europe has made his name to be associated with destruction and death.

The idea of the great king—the Lord of Man and the Lord of Death—was developed in part as a result of deaths, funerals, coffins, and unmarked graves.

Chapter *2*

Attila and the Huns

The collapse of the Western Roman Empire was one of the most important moments in human history. Many factors contributed to this event, not just one overarching or all-pervasive cause. The huge migration of Germanic peoples into the Roman Empire was the most disastrous and dramatic of these factors. Not only were they attempting to invade Rome while it was vulnerable, but they were also trying to escape the Huns, who were seen as a greater menace. They were unlike anyone the Romans had ever met.

A male Hun infant's face was seriously damaged upon birth. To make him less sensitive to pain, extensive wounds were performed on his body. As if a young son's life wasn't already difficult enough, cranial deformation was also practiced, where the infant's head was bound, giving him an elongated shape later in life. Only after this rite was over was the boy allowed to nurse with his mother. The Huns were also renowned for their unmatched proficiency with a whoreson bow, which they would have started mastering at an early age and used daily for the rest of their lives. Their cruelty was excessive even by ancient standards.

Over five hundred years earlier, on the other side of the world, began the butterfly effect of cascading events that culminated in the Roman Empire in the fourth and fifth centuries. A Great Wall was built to keep the numerous nomadic tribes of the north out of China after the warring states of China were recently united.

The numerous nomadic tribes and peoples of the north were inspired by this Chinese unification to follow suit, and the Xiongnu Confederacy was established in 209 BC. The Xiongnu were able to easily avoid the Great Wall during the early Chinese Hun Dynasty and ravage the south with impunity. The Hun Chinese were starting to pay Xiongnu regular tribute in return for not assaulting them. The two types of tribute that Xiongnu sought above and beyond silk and other opulent items were They had developed a penchant for both great quantities of wine and Chinese brides, some of whom were of noble blood. The Hun Empire did not do anything while receiving the somewhat degrading tribute during their raids in the south. They carefully examined the prejudices and tribal politics of the nascent Confederacy in turn and started to discreetly play them off against one another.

After gaining a sizable number of friends north of the great wall, the Chinese ceased paying tribute to this fledgling kingdom and instead started paying the nomads to engage in conflict among themselves and aid Chinese battles there. The success of these incredibly expensive advertising increased over time.

The Xiongnu Confederacy broke into three pieces in the first century AD. The Xiongnu in the south became a vassal of China. The Xianbei who had previously joined with a Xiongnu in the East defected and established their Confederacy. These early Mongol forefathers received a reward for each chopped head of a Xiongnu warrior they presented to the Chinese. The Hun Chinese and the Zhan Bay who captured much of their country and drove them further west handed the northern Xiongnu, who consisted of about 100 tribes and could field up to two hundred thousand soldiers, a series of catastrophic defeats.

The Xiongnu divided into several smaller but powerful coalitions of tribes that were frequently at odds with one another and the Iranian-speaking nomads they exterminated or assimilated. All of the Kidarites and Xionites relocated to the south and developed parasitic ties with the Sassanid Persian Empire. While scholars disagree on the extent to which these three tribal Confederations are related to the Huns who went west, they have all been collectively referred to as the Iranian Huns.

The Xiongnu and nearly every other prosperous Nomadic tribal confederation, including the Huns, should be noted for not being strictly racially homogeneous. The bigger outer circle of tribes that joined later had less prestige and a smaller share in the spoils of war and tribute, especially if they were forced to join. In general, the first tribes to join together to establish a nomadic coalition were the nobility.

These tribes were all dispersed over a sizable geographic area and had relationships with both the local settlers and other migratory groups. The Xionites, Kidarites, and Heptalites frequently wed Iranian language speakers and acquired a large portion of their culture. Before they started warring, the Huns that crossed the Volga River around 370 AD were initially allies with Iranian-speaking islands, and they also started assimilating Germanic peoples who had not been massacred or fled to the west into their horde. Germanic tribes that were subjugated by the Huns and thereafter joined with them in opposition to the Germanic Gods who had previously ruled them are referred to as the frightening and the keppens.

The Romans' early dealings with the Huns were not entirely negative. The Huns were immediately engaged by the Romans to solve the issue they had caused after plundering Roman land, prompting a large-scale migration of Germanic tribes into the Roman Empire, and delivering a severed head to Constantinople as a way of indicating "want to be friends."

The Huns occasionally raided Roman territory throughout the following several decades, but they were considerably more likely to fight alongside the Romans than against them. They successfully assisted in defending Italy from a gothic invasion in 406, and the Romans routinely used them as mercenaries to keep unruly German tribes in check.

Attila and Bleda, two brothers, shared leadership of the Huns in 434. The Hun leader who came before them, Ruga, kept a pact with the Romans in the West while waging war against them in the East. After that, the eastern Romans arranged a yearly bribe of 700 pounds of gold to keep Ruga away from them. During the first ten years of Attila and his brothers' rule, they largely adhered to the same policies as their uncle and placed a greater emphasis on rivalry among themselves. When Attila's brother Bleda was killed, this rivalry came to an end. At that point, Attila started his invasion of the east, prioritizing the capture of Roman engineers who he would later use to build siege machinery. The Huns could now capture fortified cities.

Eastern Romans finally had enough in 447 and consented to triple the Huns' annual contribution, to 2100 pounds of gold. Attila repeatedly called them his slave while negotiating the tribute, ridiculing them. In addition, the treaty mandated that Rome's borders be extended hundreds of miles downstream from the Danube River, stripping the Romans of their only natural defensive fortification. Attila mercilessly increased his power and control over almost the whole population of the region north of the Roman Empire in the three years that followed this treaty.

The western Roman Emperor's sister was betrothed to an elderly senator who she was not at all fond of at the time Attila had reached the pinnacle of his power, successfully establishing a vast counter-Empire to the Romans, and Attila seemed content to develop and further consolidate his Empire. History might have been very different if it weren't for her. She then had the wonderful notion to enclose a telegram pleading for assistance together with her engagement ring and send it to Attila the Hun.

All of this was seen by Attila as a more official marriage proposal, which he politely accepted and informed the

Western Roman Emperor of. He even offered to accept a sizable portion of the Western Roman Empire as a dowry. The startled and furious Western Roman Emperor initially intended to execute his sister but was persuaded by his mother to spare her life and exile her instead. Attila amassed a vast army made up of every Hun tribe in his Empire as well as a horde of German infantry to back them after being told that this was not a serious plan and to forget about the whole affair.

All of the Roman cities along the Rhine River were destroyed by Attila in 451. Some historians have asserted that Attila, allied with Rome, intended to sever his ties with the Western Roman Empire and used the engagement as justification for doing so. As Attila advanced deeper into the Empire, he continued to devastate cities, but the Roman general Flavius Aetius put together his coalition, including the Romans, the Huns' erstwhile allies, the Allens, and other Germanic tribes, including the Visigoths, Franks, and Saxons.

Attila retired to his tenth capital city in the Pannonian Basin, close to present-day Budapest, after a significant conflict between the two armies that were mainly indecisive. There, he spent the winter and plotted a new offensive. The following year, Attila launched a successful campaign of rural devastation throughout Italy. The Catholic Pope left the city to meet Attila as his army approached Rome. Roman sources claim that he was magically able to persuade Attila to spare the city. Possibly Attila spared the city because he was moved by the elderly man's valor despite being unarmed, or perhaps a bribe was offered.

In any case, Attila traveled back to his capital city, a tent city in the Pannonian Basin, where he started to plan his next military operation and wed a beautiful German Fraulein. The Hunnic Empire did not last for a very long time after Attila's death from a severe nosebleed on his wedding night, while he was severely intoxicated and unconscious. This was because Attila's children quarreled about who should control the Empire.

The Germanic tribes that were once under their control united and drove out the Huns. The Pannonian Basin served as the Huns' operational base when the Gappids founded a new kingdom there. Although the Huns' power was fleeting, their memory endured. The Magyars, who eventually came to dominate the Pannonian Basin, were nicknamed the Huns by medieval chroniclers as a slur. Attila is a significant character in three later Norse sagas.

However, they accepted the implication and asserted that they still wielded Attila's sword and carried on his heritage. Attila and the Huns have been frequently mentioned throughout history, with both positive and negative implications. Attila is still a popular name in Turkey and Hungary, where the Huns are seen as a close Turkic relative.

Chapter 3

The Scourge of God

They refer to Attila the Hun when he conquers Gneisses. He destroys anything that stands in his way. He was a killer, an extortionist, and a thug. The Attila tales are horrifying, but they originate from his rivals who have something to gain. The stories' hidden truths can now be exposed. Investigators will look for the genuine Attila by examining the circumstances surrounding his attack decision.

A psychiatrist will place Attila on the couch to determine whether he was as terrible as he is described and how he compares to other angels who have acted wrongly. Archaeological data will show how the Huns' mere presence terrified their opponents. He has a reputation for being one of history's monsters and is a raiding barbarian. Attila the

Hun is still associated with ferocity today. The behavior of Attila was examined by psychiatrists to better comprehend him. Genghis Khan and Caligula will be compared against Attila on a special Behaving Badly psychograph to show how they stack up against other historical tyrants. He has a horrifying criminal history and resembles Mother Teresa more than Hannibal Lecter. He enters a church in the French city of Reims and beheads the archbishop.

He sets out to take on this horrifying savage persona, and he succeeds in doing so. For money and gold, he destroys an entire culture, including men, women, and children. Attila terrorizes barbarians, commits mass slaughter, and plunders. He decimates the Roman army as a whole. The man is very merciless. He murders deserters in the most heinous manner conceivable.

For Attila, loyalty is everything, and he will punish treason with such brutality that it will make you wish you had never been born. The horror tales never stop, describing a degree of depravity that is impossible to comprehend. Maybe it's because they were created by his fervent adversaries, the Romans. Due to the biased nature of the data, it is very difficult to paint a true picture of the Huns. Huns are completely despised by the Romans. They are completely uninformed about the difference between good and wrong, according to the Roman author Marcellinus. a tribe of untamed people driven by the desire to plunder, rob, and kill. But can we believe the Roman historians? Attila's early years may hold some of the answers, although the documentation is hazy. According to the historian Priscus who lived during Attila's reign, the conqueror was born in or near the Hungarian region in or about 406 AD.

He is a member of the Hun Royal Family and the youngest of two brothers. He was raised in a world of meadows, tents, horses, wagons, and horse archery. Despite being the Huns' base of operations, little remains here for the archaeologists. No monuments, coins, or enduring constructions. Considering Attila's identity is highly challenging due to a lack of information and supporting data. The Romans made a crude attempt to characterize the Huns.

Political correctness wasn't their thing. The Huns are extensively described by the Roman historian Amyanise Marcellinus. He continues, "They have thick, squat, broken-bent forms; they are prodigiously ugly; and from birth, they have a ferocious love for pillaging. The children's looks are deformed by their parents. Was Attila a real-life monster from a horror film? Startling results have been obtained using hard data from specialized archaeological sites. An excavation at a GR in Hungary uncovered Attila-era Hun skulls. The malformed state of the skulls they discovered astounded them. The Huns bent their kids' skulls with a vise they had disseminated across their society.

They wrapped a bandage tightly around the baby's head after placing it on its forehead, which is why the baby's skull was misshapen. As a result, Marcellinus accurately described them, and to the Romans, their ethnic background just added to their peculiar appearance. Asians made up a sizable portion of the Hun population. This supports the claims that they were savage, strange, and horrifying when taken with the information we already have regarding the misshapen heads. Attila, who was then 28 years old, and his older brother Bleda were crowned as co-kings of the Huns in 434 AD. From the Danube River to the Baltic Sea, they seize control of a region that stretches from Germany to Central Asia.

Although there are a lot of real estate, the brothers want gold, and a lot of it, to go with it. The most reliable source is nearby, directly over the Danube. The barbarians will soon be at your gates. One Roman town after another is taken over by Attila and Bleda's soldiers, who strike quickly and vanish. According to reports, the Huns' superiority over the Romans is due to their proficiency with horses. On the saddle, these men are a force to be reckoned with as they use their arrows to attack and flee. They are attached to the saddle, arriving with lightning speed. But did Attila possess a hidden weapon, or is this just more Roman propaganda?

The saddles were different between Roman and Hun riders, though. The Huns' saddles were higher in the front and back than the Romans'. This is the saddle's advantage since all you have to do is wear it on your front, and it provides excellent back support. The rider could now turn his upper body and shoot arrows in any direction thanks to this. The key distinction is that they are practically fixed in the saddle.

When the rider is immobilized, his horse transforms into a versatile weapon platform. This is a special settle that enables us to engage in fire from all sides. This enables them to become much more adaptable and superior to their opponents, and it truly turns a pack horse or other animal into a highly developed fighting machine.

Attila develops into a terrorist of the fifth century who attacks Roman towns, raped, pillaged, killed, and set them on fire. His notoriety immediately gains a large following. This marauder must be taken seriously. However, the Romans choose to employ them as hitmen mercenaries rather than engaging in combat with Attila and his horse, demonstrating the importance of keeping your allies near and your enemies even closer. Recognizing the Huns' strength in battle, the Romans offered them immense wealth in exchange for their services.

Attila and his brother Bleda can't ignore the opportunity to kill for cash. In what is now France, in the year 437 AD, the Huns mounted a massive assault on the Burgundians. It becomes a horrible thing.

According to historical accounts, Attila massacred the rebels and turned his attention to the women and children, killing 20,000 people. But why? Is there a plan behind this hunger for blood? Attila's massacre of the Burgundians confirms the idea that his only motivation is financial gain. Its devastation is being done only out of resentment and anger.

The Romans lavishly rewarded Attila for exterminating the Burgundians, possibly unaware that they had produced a monster. After taking the gold from the Romans, Attila discovers there is much more where that came from. Once they are successful in extracting a significant reward from the Romans, they are aware that they may return for additional rewards time and time again. Attila wants a higher reward than just sacrificing animals and murdering people; the Romans are the only people he can steal that much from.

To ensure the allegiance of their Huns, Attila the Hun and his brother Bleda set out to achieve what no other barbarian had ever done—break into a defended Roman city. Rome hired Attila the Hun and his brother Bleda to perform its dirty work and paid them in gold for eliminating the Empire's adversaries. Attila essentially wants to extort money from the Roman Empire and to accomplish so, he needs to show the Roman Empire that if they don't give him the money, he's going to cause problems. He must locate a city to destroy, one like Gneisses in contemporary Serbia. Gneisses are crucial to Roman strategy in 441 AD. Even though it's a citadel with guards, there is gold inside, and Attila only cares about that. He is a plunderer, not a creator of an empire.

Attila has no interest in capturing cities; all he wants to do is knock down the gate, enter, and devastate the city before fleeing as quickly as possible. The more people he kills in the process, the better it will be for his reputation. The defending Romans slashed down Attila and his brother's horse-mounted crack warriors. According to Priscus, a Roman ambassador from Attila's time, they turn to plan B, which is as straightforward as a tree. A battering ram reportedly tore down the walls of Gneisses, according to Priscus.

Attila is not a subtle man, but could he and Bleda have created a battering ram strong enough to breach a city wall? The Ontario Provincial Police's SWAT team, which handles emergencies, will put Attila's battering ram to the test. They must first procure a ram with identical specifications as the one Attila used. According to Priscus, the tree trunk is attached to a metal cap that is held up by a covered frame. It would be covered in skins and willow-style basketry because preventing someone from throwing rocks at you while you're trying to break down their wall is one of the most crucial things you can do. The police will attempt to force their way into a factory that has cinderblock walls and steel doors.

However, the gate is frequently the most challenging point of entry when attacking a city. The strongest element of the fortification was the gate because there is where people usually try to enter. A wall that can be knocked down fully or even just a large portion of it renders the area defenseless. These eight-inch blocks are no match for the ram, but what about Roman defenses? Attila and Bleda could indeed have conquered Gneisses by breaching the Roman fortifications; nevertheless, even with this ram, we would be able to do so. Only a few Huns survived the horrific devastation they caused once they were inside.

A significant fortified city has fallen for the first time, shocking the Roman Empire. Word quickly travels that Attila is unlike any other barbarian Rome has ever encountered, and imperial towns are available for conquest.

Attila, like any terrorist, feeds on fear, so it's easy to imagine the Romans shaking in their boots as they heard rumors of him burning down houses and robbing cities. The horror reign of Attila and his brothers has only just begun. They're raising the stakes and aiming for Constantinople, the capital of the Eastern Roman Empire and the richest city in the world.

Chapter *4*

Attila conquers Constantinople

An opportunity to win a reward is perched above ancient Constantinople, the instrument of the East. Constantinople can be compared to the Fort Knox of antiquity. If Attalus wanted to acquire what he desired from it, which was more and more treasure, then it had to be split apart by him in some way. Although it was amazing to take Gneisses, Constantinople is Gneisses. Over 500,000 people live in the heavily fortified imperial city. Constantinople's walls are incredibly thick, measuring around four or five yards thick. There are various defenses besides only the walls.

The initial defensive wall, the first defensive field, the first platform where men would have been disguised, and then the main defensive wall itself are all visible from the attackers' perspective. These were the strongest defenses that existed today. But psychological warfare is Attila's great weapon, one that is much more effective than his battering ram. Long before he does, his horrifying reputation has already reached Constantinople. When Attila enters impenetrable cities, everyone perishes.

The Romans capitulate; to get Attila to go, they throw gold at him rather than relying on their defenses. We are aware of six thousand pounds of gold as one of the bribes. Three tons of gold equates to almost $100 million in current money, which is more wealth than Attila had ever experienced.

However, even 6,000 pounds of gold are insufficient for Attila. He also desires retribution. He has unfinished business with his army's deserters who are currently within Constantinople's walls. They are delivered to a dreadful end by the Romans. Because Attila is cruel, he does not welcome deserters from his army who cross over to the other side. Instead, he demands their return and eventually succeeds in getting them back. He runs them through, impales them, and hangs them up for two days till they die.

That is an Attila the Hun story. It serves as retribution for the offense of disloyalty. Who is this man to do such a thing? Attila's way of killing his enemies exhibits particularly gruesome and sadistic savagery. Nothing is safe since Attila and Bleda are so powerful that not even Constantinople can resist them. Attila is engaged in a massive protection ring organized in the mafia style. Attila is a master of strategy. He approaches the walls of Constantinople, threatens, receives his payment, and then leaves so he may return. As a result, he behaves like a mafia boss who keeps showing up and demanding money until he becomes an inseparable part of your life and culture.

Attila's blood and kin brother Bleda is the only thing standing in his way from ultimate dominance at the moment. One of history's greatest heists was carried out by Attila the Hun and his brother Bleda, who demanded gold from the Romans. The family business runs smoothly for 12 years before sibling rivalry replaces brotherly love. Bleda goes hunting one day in 445 and never returns. A Roman author named Jordanease refers to it as homicide and blames Attila for the crime. Attila and his brother shared a close upbringing, accomplished everything together, and reigned together.

Attila brutally murders him, demonstrating his psychotic murderous tendencies and establishing Attila as the only Hun leader.

Attila has amassed wealth by extorting Roman gold, which he uses to reward the loyalty of his soldiers, but the Romans have had enough. They gather an army to confront Attila on the Mitosis battlefield in present-day Bulgaria. There is complete carnage, and the only survivors are the Roman opposition. The survivors offer justifications. The Romans must defend their extermination of these barbarians, but how? It's not because they're brilliant, clever, or intelligent, though. It's because they outnumbered the meager Roman army by oceans of vastly superior forces.

According to Roman records, Attila's army totaled 500,000, compared to the Romans' 120,000, who were overwhelmed by barbarians four to one. It's a face-saving justification for the Romans, but is it accurate? It is now possible to estimate the true size of Attila's army using the knowledge of animal husbandry. It all comes down to how many horses there are. The grazing grounds of the Huns are located on the Hungarian plain, a natural sphere surrounded by the Carpathian Mountains, the Danube, and the Elves. According to studies, the grasslands of Hungary can support up to 150 000 horses. That is already considerably less than what the 500,000 Roman accounts imply.

In addition, Attila's soldiers probably possessed many horses amongst them to travel farther more rapidly. A basic army of 30,000 would be available if each Hun horseman required, say, five horses each. If the Romans wish to blame their defeat on the Huns' overwhelming size, they should come up with a stronger justification. This is a relatively small force compared to the Roman Empire. This research shows that what the Roman accounts claim is completely false.

The Romans are outnumbered four to one, not Attila. How does he manage to do it? The story by the Roman author Marcellinus contains hints. His observations of the Huns just before a tiller is born indicate that they had a distinctive strategy for fighting. He first sends in his archers to disperse the Roman forces before deploying the lasso and the net, commonplace weapons for which the Romans are unprepared. Utilizing basic tools in a highly effective manner. This would be utilized by individuals who have been designated explicitly to do so to plan a practical maneuver. Therefore, if you were to strike from one corner and one flank to the other flank, they would effectively deploy the rope in a coordinated move. The Roman infantry is then helpless in the face of lasso-throwing horsemen. Of course, dragging them there while blasting their neck would result in instant death. Tens of thousands of people perish because Rome has no response to these strategies. The Romans suffer defeat for yet another cause.

Simply said, the organized force that ruled the barbarians for generations is no longer present. The typical Roman legionary, as depicted in most Hollywood movies, is depicted as donning a helmet, a big rectangular shield intended for close combat, and a suit of armor known as lorica segment, Artur. They align their shields and begin throwing javelins at the enemy from a distance. They then charge forward while shields are locked together, draw their short swords, and stab the Huns. These were the warriors who ruled the world, but by the time of Attila, warriors like these belonged to the distant past. Roman legions during Attila's reign resembled Romans much more; in essence, he now wears barbarian-style trousers and his helmet is also based on a barbarian Persian design.

Additionally, according to the sources, the Roman army would have primarily consisted of mercenaries and barbarians who lacked the training and tools the Roman army employed to conquer the world. The Romans, crushed by their defeat, petitioned Constantinople for peace. To negotiate, an envoy travels to Attila's headquarters in Hungary. A report from Priscus, who wrote the only first-person account of Attila in history, is traveling with him.

John Man, a historian, followed the route. It takes them almost a month to go north from Constantinople, and every day Priscus discovers gruesome proof of Attila's brutality. They pass through sites that the Huns destroyed on their march south, including the town of Gneisses, which is in ruins with bones and skulls still scattered along the stream.

When they finally leave the Roman Empire and enter Attila's domain, they arrive at the Tisza River. They must have been completely terrified by what lay in wait for them. This was similar to visiting Saddam Hussein without any prior notice.

Although the precise location of Priscus's encounter with Attila is unknown, likely, they did so in a field because of the report Priscus left of him, which was somewhat startling. Priscus anticipates discovering an unclean city full of dirty barbarians, so what he discovers surprised him. In addition to wooden cabins, there was a stone bathhouse complex. Priscus notices that there is a bath complex within Attila's headquarters, which is shocking because this is a great characteristic of Roman culture and not the culture of the Huns; therefore, the presence of the bath complex there in Attila's shadow is a great indication that the Huns can adapt and adopt great Roman ideas, and the bath is one of the key characteristics of a Roman city. According to this, Attila is a typical guy who enjoys relaxing in the pool after raping and pillaging. He is also seen to be a family-oriented man.

Attila is depicted by Priscus as being an extremely well-rounded person. You can see the human side of this very stoic ruler because he is an affectionate father and Priscus recognizes his modest demeanor. How does this fit with Priscus's portrayal of Attila as a hard-drinking, hot-tempered thug who wouldn't hesitate to impale slaves and spies? The real Attila—who is he? Attila can appear to be an affluent Roman inside, but while people are being impaled outside, we discover his true nature: he is a psychopathic killer. Attila had gotten everything he can from Constantinople two years after Priscus' visit, but fortunately, the Roman Empire is divided into two. He now turns his attention to the western half of the Roman Empire after finishing the eastern half.

Chapter 5

Attila's War Against the Visigoths

Attila is back on the saddle at the age of 45, eager to defeat the Romans once more. Although it has always worked in the past, he grossly miscalculated the Empire this time. Once more on the rampage and attempting to outwit the Romans are Attila the Hun and his barbarian troops. They charge into the center of Europe galloping from the plain of Hungary. Everyone was shocked to see Attila leave his home country and travel to Central Europe after crossing the Rhine and conducting one of the most spectacular smash-and-grab raids in history.

Attila travels hundreds of miles on horseback with thousands of men, all of whom are fiery-eyed and ready for battle; in fact, they have all been fed raw meat. Uncooked flesh that has been wormed on horses is on the table, according to Roman historian Marcellinus. But even a savage has trouble digesting raw meat. This is unquestionably another instance of the Romans dehumanizing the villains. Robert Mason, a historian, was on a quest to learn more. So that we have the least amount of horse hair possible, he had a saddle blanket manufactured especially for us. The horse is ridden for six hours to see if the meat changes from repulsive to appetizing. Robert, however, has discovered that the meat has been altered in some way.

Given that it is no longer raw, it has been left with a certain amount of tenderness. Amazingly, the tale appears to be accurate. Nutritionist Lynn Weaver stated that there is the presumption that the salt on the horse and salt is a preservative, so perhaps that is preserving the exterior of the meat, keeping the bacteria at bay. To tenderize it, it was also covered and subjected to intense pressure. Due to its hard cellular structure, raw meat cannot be digested.

The pounding motion of the horse tenderizes it by disintegrating the cell walls. It's a steak tartare variation, a useful dish that allows Attila and his troops to spend more time on the saddle. The ancient city of Metz is visited by Attila and his men, which are fed on meat. The city crumbles as they unleash the battering rams. As he travels further into

Europe, he discovers deserted towns where the scared locals had fled, but the archbishop of Reims, Micaceous, remains firm and sings hymns to ward off the barbarian—though Attila is uninterested in him.

He chops off the head of that archbishop. Was Attila simply on a bloodthirsty rampage, or was there a larger plan at work here? The invasion of the Western Empire of Rome by Attila seemed to have no strategic purpose at all. It's about resentment, retaliation, wrath, and devastation.

Attila finally confronts the Roman forces of Western Europe as he arrives in the Catalonian plains in northern France.

Aetius, a Roman general, had a straightforward approach. He is aiming for group power. He combed Gaul and gathered every remaining tribe that harbored animosity toward Attila, from the surviving Burgundians to the Visigoths. It's showtime as the two armies faced off. The high ground was crucial in this conflict. The two forces were separated by a ridge of high terrain on the Catalan plain; both sides rushed to reach it first, but it was the Romans who succeeded. They just dug in on the ridge at that point and allowed Attila's cavalry to charge them from the top of the hill. Cavalry is positioned defensively against infantry. Both sides suffer severe losses.

A modern Gallic poet named Cydoniacipolla Norris claims that 100,000 soldiers perish in a single day and that the river across the plain is streaming with blood. The fact that the Huns are coming up this Ridge in waves and have been hurled back repeatedly marks a turning point.

Attila was immediately forced back into his camp after the Visigoths charged down the hill, and the unthinkable occurred: Attila lost the conflict. Instead of letting Attila employ guerilla tactics, Aegeus prevails by making him stand and engage in combat. Attila ends up being a bitter loser. Attila loses his first significant conflict. This will not serve as a deterrence. He will be enraged, seek retribution, and make an effort to make amends because he believes in pure power. Attila does exactly that; he decides Rome will pay and keeps a close eye on Italy. He traverses the Alps and begins a fresh wave of devastation. Aquileia is the fortified city that comes first. The siege equipment completes its task. Men under Attila pour into the city and obliterate it. With his terrifying reputation and ability to scare away entire populations, Attila acts as an advance scout before ultimately falling short.

According to the legend, the Pope intervenes and convinces the man to change his mind, although the truth likely has less to do with religion and more to do with how the plague is wreaking havoc on Europe. There are many reasons to go back, including famine and disease virtually certainly, so that in the end, bacteria overcame him rather than armies. Attila decides to make a wise choice and return home as the illness decimates his army and winter draws near. This hasn't been the most prosperous European trip by Attila's standards. He is still weighed down by gold that has been looted and demanded. He is about 47 years old and has lived through 19 years of brutal conflict. His hard lifestyle, not a battle, is what finally drags him down.

Attila the Hun, is destined to sow chaos. For ten years, Hitler tormented Europe and the Balkans, killing hundreds of thousands while accumulating enormous wealth. He needs some rest by 453 AD because he is exhausted, but he never gets it. He takes on a new spouse, who is lovely, fantastic, and youthful. Attila invites her into his bedroom. He's dead the following morning. Priscus claims that Attila has a nosebleed when his body is discovered. Can such a brave fighter have met such a disgraceful end? How is it possible that the Scourge of God passed away from a nosebleed? In support of his assertion that Attila died, Priscus offers medical data. Attila was discovered in a dazed state with a lot of blood on his mouth and in the vicinity of the cross, but there is no sign of vomitus. With this knowledge, a medical simulator can be used to determine the most likely cause of death. This raises the possibility that the blood entered from the digestive system or the lungs. Only little volumes of frothy blood could seep from the lungs due to tuberculosis, an infection, or a tumor. This contradicts what Priscus says. Attila had been a big drinker all of his life and may have had liver damage. The blood vessels that feed into the liver grow larger and become even more filled as a result of this.

One of the principal veins leading to the liver is reached via vessels in the throat. These vessels may burst or rupture if there is too much pressure inside of them, resulting in a significant hemorrhage. These were likely the results of his harsh life, which included excessive drinking, wild behavior, and stress. His final night of expected joy came to an abrupt end with a coughing fit, a rush of blood, and a sudden hemorrhage. The patient ends up choking on their blood, therefore in Attila's case, it was likely a mix of the shark state brought on by the severe bleeding or hemorrhage as well as the blood filling up the trachea as well as him smothering in his blood that caused his death. A violent end for a violent killer.

On the Hungary plains, Attila spent his formative years as a nomad before taking on the might of the Roman Empire. The number of dead reached hundreds of thousands. He engaged in extortionate wars of terror. He killed all the Burgundians in a violent bloodbath, committing genocide. He demolished city after city purely for the sake of doing so.

His vengeance for betrayal was horrifying, impaling a long and agonizing death, and the streets were filled with rotting bodies. Where does Attila's conduct rank among the poor behavior of the ancients? Was Attila, like Caligula, a psychopath who killed just out of passion? Or, like Genghis Khan, was he inspired to kill as part of a vision? He doesn't appear to be using violence and conquest for any particular reason. He wants to start destroying things almost just for the sake of it. He is a callous, heartless murderer. A scale of psychopathic behavior places Attila at the top. The devastation was Attila's only concern. He lacked a vision that ensured the Huns would have a future.

On a scale of originality, Attila scores quite poorly compared to the other great rulers. When in doubt, he murders. He doesn't develop anything, solve problems, or leave anything behind. You can still discover this bad psychological profile today. Attila resembles Pablo Escobar, a notorious drug lord, very much. They don't develop anything or build anything; their only interests are in raw power and money. If someone stands in their way, they kill them. Perhaps the first big terrorist in history was Attila. With the help of his protection business from the fifth century, he was able to amass immense money, but due to his lack of foresight, Attila was unable to establish the roots of a lasting civilization. It broke down after he passed away. The Huns were extinct for only thirty years before losing their whole Empire.

Chapter *6*

Battle of the Catalaunian Plains

It would be an understatement to say that the Battle of the Catalaunian Plains is Iconic. However, it is also divisive because the sources portraying the fighting are contradictory. The lack of information makes it appear as though we will never have a complete understanding of the events. Additionally, there are two imposing figures in Attila and Aetius, as well as the Great Migration.

We were forced to cover the Roman world's anguish and the creation of new kingdoms. Before their arrival on the Eurasian steppes in the latter half of the IV century, we know virtually little about the Huns. Many tribes were forced to flee to the west and enter the territory of the Roman Empire either as the allied-foederati or the invaders after they defeated the Alans and Goths, who lived to the north of the Black Sea, in the 370s. This is likely what set off a chain of events that became known as the Great Migration. The western branch of the Goths, the Visigoths, defeated the Eastern Roman army at Adrianople in 378, while Vandals Suebi first invaded Gaul before taking over a portion of Spain. Alaric's Visigoths attacked Rome in 410. Following that, in return for their military assistance against the Vandals and Suebi, the Visigoths were permitted to establish a kingdom in southern France with Toulouse as its capital. The Gepids, Alemanni, Eastern Goths, Ostrogoths, and other minor Germanic Slavic and Sarmatian tribes were also conquered by the Huns at this time.

They invaded the Balkans, the Caucasus, Northern Iran, and Eastern Anatolia between 395 and 399, making raids against both the Eastern Roman and Sassanid Empires. Due to the tremendous decentralization of the Hunnic kingdom, many of its warriors worked as mercenaries for both the Western Romans and the Goths. The Eastern Roman Empire was still the target of invasions, and in 422, the Empire was compelled to pay a yearly tribute. The Western Empire was also experiencing issues as a result of internal conflicts, uprisings, and additional invasions. Enter Flavius Aetius, a Roman general who may have had Scythian or Gothic ancestry. He was held captive at the Visigoth and Hunnic courts as a kid, where he learned much about their warfare techniques and made key allies among the Huns. It enabled him to gather a sizable Hunnic force in 423 and travel to Italy to help Joannes succeed on the throne.

However, another impostor, Valentinian, had already been crowned by the time Aetius arrived in Ravenna, the city's capital. Aetius was given a sizable quantity of money and made the commander in Gaul to quell his ambitions. Despite several failures, he succeeded in restoring Roman power to the majority of Gaul by using Hun mercenaries. He relocated the Alans near Orleans to quell the uprising in Brittany, overthrew the Burgundian monarchy and relocated it to the south, weakened the Visigoths, and weakened the Franks, effectively establishing his semi-independent kingdom in the area.

Ruga, the first centralized Hun state's monarch, died in 433 and was succeeded by his nephews Attila and Bleda. The agreement between the new rulers and the Eastern Romans was renegotiated in 435, and in exchange for a vow not to form an anti-Hunnic alliance, they received 700 pounds of gold annually. This calm, though, was fleeting. Carthage was taken prisoner by the Vandals in 439. The Eastern Roman Empire dispatched an invasion to retake Africa the next year. Between 441 and 443, the Huns raided and pillaged the

Balkans, and this time they even made it to Constantinople, thanks to the Sassanids' onslaught on the Romans in the East. Emperor Theodosius was compelled to consent to a yearly payment of 6,000 pounds. In 445, Attila, who would later govern the Hunnic realm, killed Bleda. Attila again invades the Eastern Romans in 447; the reason for this is unknown. At the Battle of the Utus, he routed the Roman soldiers. He then invaded the Balkans and forced the emperor to sign another truce, this time promising to leave the Danube region as a buffer.

Around that period, Attila and Aetius's friendship deteriorated. Various sites offer various justifications: Aetius was made weaker since the Huns couldn't work as mercenaries. At the same time, one of the Frankish successors and the Vandals, who had enmity with the Visigoths, encouraged Attila to invade Gaul to deal with their adversaries. Honoria, the sister of the Western Roman Emperor, asked Attila for assistance by sending him her ring; however, he mistook it for a vow of marriage and is said to have demanded half of the Empire as a dowry. In contrast to other allies, the Huns did not acquire any areas within the Roman Empire, which infuriated Attila.

Surprisingly, the Eastern Romans' refusal to provide tribute in 450 led to the outbreak of war against the Western Roman Empire. Attila realized the Balkans were devastated and had little chance of capturing Constantinople, so he chose to invade Gaul instead because he needed the money to pay his forces. Attila crossed the Rhine in the spring of 451 with the assistance of the Ostrogoths, Gepids, Alemanni, and others. Aetius was in Italy at that time and was unable to rely on his customary Hunnic units, so he was compelled to ally with his opponent, Theodoric, king of the Visigoths, beg the Burgundians and Franks for assistance, and hastily travel to Gaul.

Almost nothing is known about the movement of Attila's army or the cities that they captured, but by early June, his horse-heavy army had arrived at Orleans. The sources differ; some contend that Attila besieged the city and was compelled to end it when Aetius quickly arrived in the region, while others believe that because Aetius was close to Orleans before the Huns, Attila was unable to blockade the city. Additionally, it is unknown if Sangiban, the leader of the Alani, intended to support either the Huns or the Romans or if he was simply waiting to see which side would prevail. In any case, the Huns withdrew since the terrain was unfavorable for the cavalry, and Alani joined Aetius, who had also received reinforcements from Visigoths, Franks, Burgundians, and Saxons.

At that point, the Roman general started after Attila. Although the precise location of the battle, which is more commonly known as the Battle of the Catalaunian Plains, is unknown, some contemporary historians have concluded that it took place in the area now known as Maurica, close to Troyes, about 200 kilometers from Orleans, and not close to Chalons as was previously believed. The amount of troops is another widely contested subject, but it's plausible that both sides had about 40,000 fighters. The Roman army had more infantry than their adversaries', whilst the Hunni army was heavily cavalry-heavy with elite horse archers at its core. For two weeks, Aetius followed Attila.

On June 19, his Frankish vanguard engaged Attila's Gepid rearguard in combat, but the Gepids quickly withdrew because Attila wanted to lure the Romans to a location that would benefit his cavalry. The Romans had to divide their troops in two to go through the woodland that was dividing the two paths leading to Maurica, but Attila did not attempt to block them at the chokepoints, perhaps correctly believing that his infantry was inferior to the enemy.

On the Montgueux ridge, a small cavalry force was still present. The Visigothic column encountered this detachment on the hill early on June 20. Attila sent some additional cavalry to the crest despite not intending to defend this position in favor of engaging the Romans on the adjacent wide field to the east. The initial unit and the reinforcements both advanced gradually while firing a few volleys. The Visigoths had taken control of the ridge by the afternoon, and despite both sides having strong defensive positions, the troops began to deploy because they required decisive combat. To prevent Attila from attacking the Romans from the sides or the back, Aetius formed his army with his right flank protected by the aforementioned ridge, his rear and left flank by the forests, and a small cavalry detachment under Theodoric's son Thorismund on the ridge so the summit would conceal them. To build a shield wall with archers in the second line, Theodoric and the Visigoths dismounted while holding the right wing.

The Romans, Franks, Burgundians, and Saxons maintained the left flank with infantry in the first line forming a shield wall, another group of missile infantry behind them, and the Alan cavalry in the rear. The Alan cavalry took the middle. While Valamir-led Ostrogoth cavalry manned the left flank and other Germanic infantry followed them, Attila and his Huns, who were all mounted, took up the middle. Attila positioned Ardaric on the right, followed by more Germanic troops in the second line, and the Frank infantry and Gepid cavalry. After making a speech in front of his troops, the Hun leader arranged his horse archers into a wedge shape in the middle. The Alans responded in kind as the Huns advanced, but Sangiban's horsemen were forced to flee due to the Huns' overwhelming numerical advantage. The Hun wedge then split down the middle, moving to the left and the right, firing arrows at the Romans and Visigoths, although these volleys were less successful due to the shield wall's resistance. On the other hand, the second line's missile units succeeded in wounding and killing a large number of weakly armored Huns.

However, when the Gepids pushed against the Romans, this offensive covered the Ostrogoth advance against their Visigoth counterparts. Both shield walls were initially forced back, but as the cavalry's momentum waned, the shield walls regained their composure, allowing the second line of archers to keep firing arrows above the shields. The Huns, however, turned back towards the center and attempted to enter the gap created by the Alan retreat. That posed a flanking and rear threat to the Visigoth shield wall.

The fight appeared to be going in Attila's favor until the Visigoth ruler Theodoric was murdered while trying to inspire his troops. Even yet, Aetius was able to divert some of the Alans and order them to plug the center together with the cavalry reserves, which helped to stop the tide. Feeling that victory was imminent, Attila sent in his second line of soldiers. When Thorismund saw his father had passed away, he eventually descended from the ridge and charged the enemy's left flank and rear. It appears that the Hunnic remnants were surrounded and obliterated. Attila gave the order to retire to the camp after realizing that his cavalry was snarled up and his right was making little progress against the Romans. The conflict came to an end by dusk. It is puzzling why Aetius did not launch an attack the following day given that the Huns appeared to be in trouble.

According to some historians, the Visigoths and Franks chose not to engage in battle, while other sources contend that Aetius himself was reluctant to eliminate the Huns because they provided the perfect counterbalance to the Germanic nations.

According to a later Frankish narrative, Attila gave Aetius money. The following day, the Hun army nonetheless marched away from the region in the direction of Pannonia. We will likely never know the exact toll, but even if it were high, Attila invaded the Roman Empire once more in 452, this time via Italy, and ravaged Aquileia and Milan, unintentionally forcing the establishment of Venice. Again, we don't know why, but reports claim that he turned around after speaking with Pope Leo.

In 453, Attila either passed away from a disease or was murdered by his young wife. The Hun Empire was destroyed when Attila's sons were routed by the Gepids of Ardaric in the battle of Nedao a year later. Aetius is assassinated in the same year by Emperor Valentinian, who is later killed in 455 by Aetius' bodyguards. The Western Roman Empire is over in just 20 years. The Roman Empire has struggled to keep its unity since the latter half of the fourth century AD.

Widespread social turmoil, civil conflict, and the massive migration of people from the far side of the Rhine and Danube rivers all occurred during this time. Numerous Germanic warbands and tribes, each numbering 10 to 20,000 people, spilled across the border after being pushed west by nomads from the Asian steppe. Others went in search of plunder while others sought safety. There wasn't much that could be done in the West to impede the invasion of Roman territory. Over a century of economic disintegration that wiped out the main political, cultural, and economic forces that kept the Empire together drained the government.

The Imperial Army gradually lost strength as a result of these bad economic policies, becoming a mere ghost of what it once was. The crisis also brought about punitive taxes on the poor, which bound the masses to the wealthy's holdings. Due to the weight of the people, many decided it would be preferable to rebel and go rogue or sell themselves into slavery. Rome lacked the resources necessary to combat its longtime foes when the strain along the frontier grew too high, which caused the Frontier system to completely collapse. New kingdoms in Hispania and Northern Africa defied the Empire while the Province of Britain was lost and the majority of Gaul was conquered. Rome was on its last legs after years of slow degeneration. Even worse, nomads from the East followed closely behind the Germanic tribes, posing a fire and sword threat to the Empire. The Huns were they. The Hunnic domain stretches from the Rhine to the Pontic steppe in the year 423 AD.

These wandering warriors left a path of untold destruction in their wake, leaving countless cities and regions in ruins. They seemed impossible to defeat or protect against because of their sudden appearance. The Huns were dominated by Ruga in the east and Octar in the west at this time. The Hunnic realm reached its geographical peak during their rule. And after Octar's passing in 430, it is said that Ruga proved to be a capable leader, successfully concentrating the tribes and turning the Huns into a war machine that terrorized Europe. Hunnic raids had a particularly negative impact on the Eastern Empire. As he frequently had to deal with Sassanid Persia as well, Emperor Theodosius II thought it more practical to pay an annual tribute of 350 pounds of gold in exchange for peace. But the situation in the West was just as worrying.

With his passing in the middle of August, Theodosius' uncle Emperor Honorius ended a 30-year turbulent reign that was primarily to blame for the Western Empire's decline. A high-ranking officer named Joannes was chosen as his replacement by important elites because he left no heir. He was not, however, acknowledged by the court at Constantinople because he was not a member of the Theodosian dynasty. Emperor Theodosius wasted no time in organizing a military campaign to install his cousin, young Valentinian III, as king of the western world. Illyricum was given to the Eastern Empire as a result of his support for the boy, though. Knowing that war was imminent, Joannes ordered a certain Aetius to petition the Huns for military assistance.

Flavius Aetius was raised for imperial service and was born into a wealthy family. He spent a portion of his early adulthood as a "hostage" of the Huns, a position of immense significance that helped the barbarians and the Empire forge political and diplomatic ties. Aetius made close relations with the Hunnic ruling class while he was there. He was crucial in forging the alliances that allowed the Western Empire to enlist the lucrative Hun mercenaries while the Hunnic Kings loaded their coffers with tribute, allowing the Western Empire to enroll them. Most crucially, Aetius's connections turned into a useful political resource.

Influential Romans relied on him to supply barbarian forces when they needed to further their political careers, in addition to asking him for counsel on how to deal with the barbarians. Similar to Joannes, who required an army to maintain his hold on the throne, Aetius was recruited and used his connections with the Hunnic court to bring back an army of horsemen. But he was unable to arrive in time.

The Eastern Roman army overthrew Joannes and put Valentinian III in power in May 425 after a bloody campaign and a healthy dose of treason. Aetius' current situation was unusual. He had committed treason by marching against the legitimate emperor of the Theodosian dynasty. The cunning general nonetheless used the Hunnic army at his back as a political trump card. Galla Placidia, the imposing mother of the young emperor and the real heir apparent during Valentinian's minority, realized quickly that Aetius could depose her son and decided it would be prudent to not only drop all treason charges against him but also give him command over Gaul and pay for his Hunnic troops.

Ruga, whose tribes were thought to be under his control and had fled into Roman territory, started a campaign against the Eastern Empire from the plains across the Danube at the same time. However, he passed away a few months into the campaign; some say he was struck by lightning, while others claim he died of the plague. Whatever the case, replacing such a capable leader would have been challenging, and Theodosius hoped that the barbarians would dissipate now that Ruga was no longer in charge. Indeed, as tribes to the east and north-east gradually slipped from their control in the years following his death, the decentralized Hunnic domain's influence gradually shrank. By the time his nephews Bleda and Attila succeeded to the throne, the Hunnic realm's core was located in Pannonia, with its main centers of influence being the Germanic, Sarmatian, and Slavic tribes in the region. Despite this, the Huns continued to have a significant influence on Roman politics by dominating the region.

The two brothers showed an equal capacity for adaptation to the fast-paced, constantly-evolving Late Roman era. They coerced Theodosius into signing an unsatisfactory peace in 435 to put an end to Ruga's campaign. Hunnic businessmen were given access to markets in Roman cities, the annual payment paid to the Huns was doubled to 700 pounds of gold, and Theodosius was forced to hand over famous Hunnic fugitives, including two of royal descent who were later executed by Attila for accepting Christianity. While growing up, Bleda and Attila lived a life far from the hardships typically associated with nomadic tribes despite being born into the most powerful Hunnic family.

Instead, they lived a life identical to that of the Roman aristocracy.

They were well-educated in royal intrigue and military and diplomatic strategy, and they could read, write, and speak Gothic and Latin. They also received skilled instruction in archery, sword fighting, lasso use, horse riding, and grooming, much like all Huns of royal blood. It appears that Attila held sway over the western portions while Bleda presided over the valued eastern wing, where he pushed the center of Hunnic territorial dominance towards the Rhine.

Early in his reign, Attila kept up the lucrative partnership with Aetius, and he and his brother would continue to help the Roman army militarily for many more years. Aetius granted Attila the honorary title of magister militum in exchange for the Hunnic king's support in defeating the two Theodosian emperors, and in return, the Hunnic king received a generous salary and a steady supply of grain for his army. Attila also received some of Pannonia. The Roman general then took immediate action to increase his strength.

In a series of civil wars, he defeated his Roman rivals by assassinating them and enlisting the help of the Huns, further destabilizing the West. Gaiseric, king of the Vandals, took advantage of the internal power struggle in Rome to cross from Hispania, invade Roman Mauretania, fortify his position in the Province of Africa, and eventually conquer Carthage in 439. Gaiseric's control over the region he had conquered was recognized by a contract that Aetius was able to arrange in return for grain supplies and yearly tribute to Rome. But he had no desire to truly take back Africa. When the Britons were attacked by the Picts and other barbarians, similar to the north of Britain, which was still nominally a member of the Empire, their cries for assistance went unanswered. Instead, Aetius made it the cornerstone of his strategy to preserve Roman Gaul. In a series of military encounters over the years, he successfully stopped the Visigoths' advance by driving them back to their possessions in Aquitania.

Using their cavalry to reinforce his armies, he routed the Franks and Alans in the north and enrolled them as foederati of the Empire. Rebels in Raetia and Noricum were brutally put down, and Roman power was reinstated north of the Alps along the Danube. He then routed a Burgundian force close to the Middle Rhine and consented to peace. However, he betrayed the agreement just a year later by inviting Attila's Huns to cross the border and exterminate the Burgundians.

Tens of thousands were slaughtered, and a few years later, Aetius forcibly relocated the survivors to the south, ultimately weakening the Burgundian realm. Armorica, a haven for brigands, immigrants fleeing the unrest in Britain, poor peasants, fugitive slaves, and deserters, all united together in open hostility to the Roman proto-feudal exploitation, put down a significant revolt of the Bagaudae rebels. The constantly unstable area remained a concern, depleting manpower continuously.

Aetius relocated the Alans along the Loire Valley to free up his men, giving them the responsibility of containing the Bagaudae in the north and pressuring the Visigoths in the south. Aetius was now acknowledged as being the most powerful man in the West. He protected Gaul as if it were his fiefdom, at the expense of all other parts of the Western Empire, from both internal and external dangers. The Vandals launched an assault after realizing Rome had invested its resources in Gaul.

First, Gaiseric wed the daughter of Visigothic King Theodoric to his son Huneric. Not only could such an alliance defeat the Western Empire, but it would also cut off Africa's grain supply and trade income. The Empire would be helpless if Aetius was unable to pay his soldiers. Gaiseric afterward invaded Sicily in 440. Vandal troops were now sent to Italy by the conquered Roman ports and ships in Africa. The Roman world was concerned about reports of barbarians streaming over the Mediterranean. Theodosius sent out a sizable armada to subdue the Vandals a year later. However, the Emperor had to mobilize substantial forces from outside the Imperial limits to launch the expedition, and Rome's neighbors had taken notice. Sassanid soldiers invaded from the east. Before Theodosius consented to pay tribute, nearly two years of small-scale combat ended indecisively but contributed to the depletion of Rome's resources. The Huns invaded once more on the Danube boundary in 441. This time, walled cities weren't an issue. Attacks were mounted using mobile towers, scaling ladders, and battering rams. As the major Balkan city centers were one by one reduced to ruins, the Huns distinguished themselves from other tribal armies by their capacity to capture walled cities. Attila and Bleda left for home in 442 after conveying Theodosius their demands after amassing more loot than they could carry.

The peace offer was, however, turned down by the Emperor. To finance the fight against the Huns, he ordered the troops from Sicily to be recalled as well as the mass minting of new coins. The Huns launched yet another campaign in 443. Major fortified metropolitan centers suffered severe damage, and whole populations were either massacred or sold into slavery.

A Roman army outside of Constantinople was wiped out by Attila and Bleda, who traveled as far south as Thermopylae in Greece. Behind its fortifications, the Eastern city was secure, while a second Roman force was routed close to Kallipolis. The annual tribute was tripled to 2,100 pounds in gold, and the ransom for each Roman soldier taken prisoner was established at 12 solidi. Theodosius, who was unable to handle the onslaught, filed a lawsuit for peace and was humiliated in the process. Bleda reportedly perished in 445, possibly the victim of an assassination, when the Huns withdrew back into their domain. The Huns were now ruled solely by Attila. The Visigothic-Vandal alliance was successful in the West. They captured southern Sicily and restrained Roman forces in Gaul. They would eventually conquer the Empire; it was only a question of time. Political squabbling undoubtedly did not improve Rome's situation.

Even though Valentinian had grown, he was still simply the nominal emperor with little authority outside of Italy. However, he made use of his meager influence to stop Aetius from receiving support in his battle against the barbarians, who were angry at the general's unrestricted authority. As usual, Aetius openly manipulated the imperial system. To strengthen his position in Gaul, he advocated the union of Gaiseric's son and Valentinian's daughter through an alliance with Gaiseric. It was a wise decision. He was well aware that Theodoric's daughter was already married to Gaiseric's son, and that if his proposal were accepted, it may cause the Vandals and the Visigoths to sever their alliance. The plan succeeded.

Gaiseric couldn't resist the offer from Aetius. He would now have time to strengthen his control over his newly acquired territory and restore his overworked forces. More importantly, it was impossible to pass up the chance to marry his son Huneric into the Roman royal line. The fact that Huneric was already wed to Theodoric's daughter didn't bother the Vandal King much. He hacked off her nose and ears before returning her to Theodoric after accusing her of attempting to poison him to get rid of her. An end was made to the Visigothic-Vandal alliance. Aetius was progressively letting up control of the situation in Hispania to the west.

Nevertheless, he plotted to keep the Visigoths occupied by offering them land south of the Pyrenees in exchange for helping Rome put down a Bagaudae uprising in Tarraconensis and weaken the Suebi, who had by this point significantly increased their dominance on the peninsula. Although the mission was unsuccessful, it was successful in keeping a sizable Visigothic force out of Aetius' territories in Gaul. His two-pronged diplomatic effort, which he launched in 447 to disarm both the Vandals and the Visigoths, was a genuine political coup. Aetius resumed his devious plans in Italy by tying his son to Valentinian's younger daughter.

Additionally, this improved Emperor Marcian's standing within the Empire in 450. He promptly changed his indecisive predecessor's catastrophic tribute policy and implemented a stronger one toward the Huns. Under his authority, be a more determined adversary. Despite being enraged, Attila did not renew and started getting ready for a fight with his childhood friend and comrade. Good, however, his house's legitimacy would significantly increase if he married into the Theodosian dynasty. However, storm clouds were forming in the east. The Huns again crossed the Danube in 447. Poor harvests for two years, plague outbreaks, and a slew of earthquakes wreaked havoc across the Eastern Empire, forcing Theodosius to stop giving the yearly tribute. Attila then arrived to get what he was owed. This time, he focused on Constantinople, whose walls had suffered significant damage in the powerful earthquakes earlier in the year. The populace hurried to restore the defenses while an army marched out to confront the invaders. However, the Romans lost badly near the river Utus, though not before inflicting significant deaths on the invaders.

Without any resistance, the Huns decimated Thrace, leaving some cities so devastated that they remained abandoned until the reign of Justinian, some 70 years later. But in time, Constantinople's walls were restored. Once more, Attila was forced to retreat by the city's strong fortifications. Theodosius, however, was once more compelled to pay the Huns for peace and consented to give up much of the lower Danube frontier as a buffer wasteland. Attila used the forced surrender of territories that had been under the Empire's rule for decades to remind everyone of his might and prowess in securing concessions from the Romans. But as soon as Theodosius passed away and Marcian became the new Eastern Emperor in 450, everything changed. He instantly changed his indecisive predecessor's ruinous tribute payment to a firmer policy toward the Huns. The extensive military preparations of the new emperor made it evident that the East would be a more tenacious foe under his rule. Attila was enraged but chose not to escalate the conflict. The Hunnic king instead headed west. He prohibited the Hun mercenaries from working for Rome and started getting ready for a fight with his buddy and childhood friend.

Aetius and Attila's cordial relationship was coming to an end, and the Roman general would no longer be able to rule Gaul with an iron fist thanks to the Huns. There are various explanations put up for Attila's abrupt change in course, while it is not apparent why he severed long-standing diplomatic ties with the West. Regardless of his motivations, a direct assault on Rome ran the risk of alienating the barbarian friends who made up the majority of his army. He needed two reasons to start a war, and he found them. One was the recent death of the Frankish King Chlodio, which led to a power struggle between his sons and the division of the kingdom, with one son turning to Aetius for help and the other to Attila. But there wasn't enough justification for all-out war in the Frankish internal conflict. The other was Justa

Grata Honoria, the aspirational sister of Valentinian. When her plot to kill the emperor and take over was discovered, she was forcibly wed to a senator who supported the monarch so that he could keep an eye on her. She even sent a letter and a ring to Attila, pleading with him to spare her from an undesirable marriage. Attila decided to read this as a marriage proposal even though it might not have been one. He agreed and requested the Western Empire's share as dowry. Valentinian rejected Attila's demands and contested the marriage proposal. The Hunnic ruler needed a pretext, and this provided it. The war had commenced.

Chapter 7

Attila invades the Western Roman Empire

Attila argued that by advancing into the West, he was not an invading force but rather a man asserting his claim to be the emperor's upcoming in-law. With Honoria as his wife, the Hunnic monarch would have the chance to conquer Gaul and carry on the West's support for its allies while also gaining territory inside the Empire and a straight line to the throne.

Aetius was taken off guard in a way that he had rarely, if ever, been. He left Italy for Gaul after learning about the approaching invasion. Aetius brought the Auxilia Palatina, but Valentinian provided very little assistance. These were elite soldiers, though few, who could carry out more mobile operations in addition to standing their ground in the line of battle. However, Aetius lacked the manpower to repel the invaders even when he merged them with his main force in Gaul. The Roman general appeared to be facing an impossible challenge. He relied on the Huns and Alans for more than 20 years to impose his power over the Visigoths, Franks, Burgundians, and Bacaudae. But now that Attila was approaching, he was forced to ask his foes for assistance. Theodoric could never be convinced to join him, but the ever-ingenious Aetius asked Avitus for help. The Visigothic King's personal friend and closest advisor was a renowned Roman aristocrat named Avitus, who had held the position of Praetorian Prefect of Gaul. He urged Theodoric not to settle old political scores with Aetius at this time. The time has come for him to join forces with the Romans to thwart Attila. As a result of diplomacy and charm, the monarch was persuaded to march out of his city, assembling a force capable of taking on the largest barbarian army to have ever threatened the Roman Empire. The union with Theodoric was, however, a marriage of convenience for Aetius.

He had no wish to see the Visigoths' authority increase, but he was compelled to seek assistance and would have to make concessions to them. He intended to halt Attila while also maintaining his position as the most powerful warlord in Gaul. He also intended to hinder Theodoric from taking advantage of any triumph over the Huns. Frankish contingents from the north arrived to join the Huns as they crossed the Rhine in the spring of 451. To make foraging easier, Attila divided his army into smaller bands and concentrated his forces only close to fortified towns. Invading and taking control of a city would have provided his army with loot, slaves, and more supplies. When faced with well-fortified cities, he was unable to pay the time required for siege operations and was forced to depend solely on fear to gain access by offering to spare the populace from a horrifying sack in exchange for food and shelter. And Attila would likely have continued to move had the gates not been opened. Early in April, the Hunnic army seized Metz and destroyed it before slicing a swath through the countryside. The invaders faced almost no resistance because there were no organized Roman standing armies. Their movement was more governed by logistics than by tactical concerns. Attila was required to allow his followers to plunder, but his priority would have been to move rapidly and cause enough trouble that Aetius would have to file a peace suit. His destination was the crucial strategic city of Aurelianum.

Gaul would have been divided in half by taking it, but if that wasn't enough to persuade the Romans to negotiate, he could engage them in battle, defeat them, and demand concessions as he had in the East. Sangiban, the chief of the Alans, must have heard about the impending Huns. He probably sought to play a cunning game to align himself with the team that stood the best chance of succeeding. Although there is some disagreement on his allegiance, it seems likely that he supported Aetius from the start given their successful partnership over the years.

Whatever the case, Attila was unaware of a Romano-Visigothic coalition that may pose a threat to him. What's worse, Aetius arrived in Aurelianum first. He quickly fortified the city's periphery and turned it into a gathering place for the northern soldiers. With the help of the Bacaudae and the recent British immigrants, the crafty general struck a contract that promised them independence from imperial rule in exchange for their allegiance. Smaller Sarmatian Celtic Swabian and German tribes, as well as the Olibriones (who were former Roman soldiers), and the Alans from the Loire valley, were persuaded to join. Other Frankish, Auxiliary, and Saxon contingents of outlaws from Armorica, Liticians, and Burgundians, as well as smaller Sarmatian Celtic tribes, were also persuaded to join.

Attila realized that the Romans were in a better defensive position at Aurelianum once he got there. There is some evidence to suggest that the fact that he was facing Aetius' unified army on adverse woodland terrain near the Loire unnerved him. The Hunnic king left Aurelianum as a result. He might have anticipated capturing the city without a struggle, but when this became impossible, he was forced to engage in combat and desired to do it in a location of his choosing. The flat Catalaunian Fields would benefit his troops because he was aware of the terrain he had already traversed after crossing the Rhine. The infantry would have traveled cross-country via the Forest of Orleans with Senones serving as their rallying point, while mounted contingents and the baggage train would have stayed on the route. After having to wait a few days, Aetius finally left Aurelianum once all of his reinforcements had shown up. He estimated that it would take him around eight days to catch up to Attila before the latter could cross the Seine. In the steep, densely forested area where the Huns had little opportunity to maneuver, the Roman general sent out fast-moving contingents of horsemen ahead of the main army to harry Attila's column. Attila didn't sustain many casualties as a result, but it did make resupplying his forces more challenging because the Roman allied army had ample supplies.

Attila's approach was further slowed down by a significant fight between Aetius' Franks and the Hunnic column's rear, allowing Aetius to catch up. Due to this, Attila had to abandon a sizable rearguard of Gepids so that the main army could take up position on the plains in front of them. The moral of the Hunnic army would have been low after the retreat from Aurelianum and having to repel ambushes and skirmishing attacks for the previous ten days. Attila faced the additional problem of boosting morale by promising his followers that they would take a stand and beat the Romans in the advantageous terrain immediately ahead. As Attila approached the wide Catalaunian pastures, he faced a choice. His army was worn out, and he was on the defensive.

He had two options: risk losing everything by engaging in combat or flee to fight another day. Knowing that an army fleeing through hostile territory was like a diseased herd and easy prey, the Hunnic monarch was mindful that there might not be another day. Even worse, fleeing from an approaching adversary was not how a warrior lived, and it was certainly not how a leader of his stature could maintain control over the several tribal warlords he was in charge of. He'd go up against the Romans.

Attila deployed a cavalry detachment to take a ridge overlooking the valley as June 19 drew to a close after immediately realizing its significance. In the distance, he set up camp on the banks of the Seine, with a wagon fort in the front and a bridge in the back that would serve as a crucial escape route over the river in the event of trouble. With 7 miles of flat, wide plains extending as far as the eye could see to the southwest, the Huns would have had advance notice of the enemy's arrival. His soldiers would get a nice night's sleep tonight. Early on June 20th, a comet was seen menacingly slicing through the sky, seemingly heralding the start of the fight. Aetius then showed up shortly after. The

Roman general had divided his force into two columns and had arrived at around 7 a.m., just as Attila had expected. Aetius wished to leave as soon as possible in the morning. He required a swift, successful conflict. If they got engaged in a long war of attrition, the group of his allies would scatter back to their homes. The Hunnic ruler started assembling his army after hearing from his scouts that the Romans were approaching. Importantly, he dispatched yet another cavalry unit to support the Hunnic riders on the mountain to the south.

Attila preferred to begin the conflict as late in the day as possible, in contrast to Aetius. He would be able to regroup in the cover of the night if he could wait until there were only a few hours left before dusk in case the Romans gained the upper hand. Aetius did not wish to leave a Hunnic contingent in his rear, as he had predicted. The Roman general ordered the Visigothic cavalry commander Thorismund to capture the ridge as the rest of the army advanced toward the battleground. The Huns stayed back as the Visigoths advanced up the slope. They gently withdrew while arrowing the opposition. Thorismund's progress was hindered by the harassment as the swift horsemen continued to flee to safety. Attila preferred to battle on the level plain below, which was more advantageous for his army, rather than for possession of the heights.

His plan to station his cavalry on the ridge was to obstruct Aetius' progress and delay his deployment. And it appeared that Attila's stalling strategies were successful. The Visigoths didn't take control of the heights until 11 a.m., four hours after the Roman army first entered the battle. Aetius anchored his right flank on the rising slope to the south and his left wing on the dense forest to the north rather than going toward the center of the field where he would be exposed to encirclement by the swift-moving Huns.

Aetius attempted to create his backup plan, much like Attila, by creating his line at the bottom of the steep meadow that rose to the high lands behind him. If he lost the battle, he would have been able to flee up a hill where it would have been challenging for the mounted Huns to pursue him. The right-wing was occupied by Theodoric and the Visigoths. To defend themselves against the Hunnic archers, the majority of them dismounted and formed a shield wall. The King himself oversaw the tiny cavalry unit that remained in reserve. In the center-right corner were the mounted Alans. Aetius might have sought to encircle the Alan leader with a large number of devoted soldiers because he may have had doubts about Sangiban's commitment to the cause.

The Alans fought on horseback like the Huns, not constructing a shield wall like the rest of the battle array. Center-left, Aetius assumed control. The Roman infantry, which included Franks, Burgundians, Saxons, and other allied tribes, extended from there to the left wing. The vast majority built a shield wall like the Visigoths. To fill any gaps in the line, two cavalry contingents were kept in reserve. Attila watched Aetius' defensive positioning in the meantime. No envelopment would be feasible because the Roman formation was hidden beneath the slope and the majority of the soldiers were surrounded by a shield wall.

Although the frontal assault was the only choice given by Aetius' deployment, Attila had never lost a war before, and he was fighting on a field of battle he had chosen. He did, after all, cross the Rhine to engage in battle with the Romans. His opportunity to defeat them was now. His Huns, who made up the bulk of his force, took up position in the middle. Ostrogothic cavalry gathered in front on the left wing. Germanic footmen, including the Burgundians, Thuringians, Alammani, Rugians, and Heruls, were arranged in the second line. Frankish infantry and Gepid cavalry were deployed on the right flank, with a second force of mixed Germanic infantry deployed in the rear.

A rallying point for the cavalry and reinforcement for any assaults were provided by the second line of Germanic infantry on each flank. Attila was successful in delaying Aetius' deployment just as he had intended. There were only 5 to 6 hours left before sunset. The time had come. Attila intended to concentrate his assault on the less-powerful Roman center-right. He would have known that the position of the mounted Alans was Aetius' line's weakest point, and he planned to exploit it. To buy him time to defeat the Alans, he ordered the Franks and Gepids on the right and the Ostrogoths on the left to bind the Romans and Visigoths. The Huns launched their assault in waves to maximize the power of their bowfire. The barbarians appeared to have dispersed into smaller groups on purpose, scurrying about in chaos, to the average Roman soldier. The Visigoths and the Roman center-right were the targets of Attila's volleys to support the mounted attack on the wings, but the Alan contingent took the brunt of the hail of arrows. He sought to weaken and disperse Aetius' ranks before the Ostrogoths, Franks, and Gepids started their charge since he was aware that a cavalry charge could fail against hardy infantry.

Hours went by as the Hunnic onslaught didn't let Aetius' troops rest. The Romans and Visigoths, hiding behind their shields, must have experienced tremendous physical and psychic damage. The Alans began firing back with their barrages, but because they were mounted and motionless, they were much easier to hit, and as their losses mounted, gaps started to form in their line. Attila gave the command for a broad charge after determining that the concentrated arrow volleys had damaged their fortitude. The Hunnic wedged formations crashed into the Alans, slicing right through their formation, on a very narrow front. When the Alans were overpowered, some of them held on while others fled, creating a chasm that divided the Roman army in two. Theodoric and Aetius desperately tried to close the center gap and halt the breakthrough by turning their cavalry contingents.

The shock of the Hunnic charge forced the opposition back and bent their battle lines inward on either side of the chasm. Attila's Germanic infantry then joined the assault, giving it even more momentum. The warriors at the front engaged in close combat while shielded, thrusting spears and swords into the adversary. The battle swung back and forth on the Roman left, but the mixed allied infantry was able to halt the Gepid and Frankish advance. The united charge of the Huns, Ostrogoths, and mixed Germanic infantry, on the other hand, heavily pressured the Visigoths on their right flank. The news that King Theodoric had been killed in battle while rousing his troops then reached Aetius.

The Roman general signaled to Thorismund, understanding that this was a crucial period in the conflict. The Visigothic cavalry rushed down the slope from where they had been concealed behind the hill's crest up to this point. Attila's Germanic infantry was preparing to form a line against the approaching cavalry when they were caught off guard. They

83

had no time, however, to hastily create a shield wall and were defeated. Aetius was able to gather the Alans in the middle and maintain the line. After failing in his attempt to stomp out the Roman center, Attila's offensive stopped. The Ostrogoths fled the field as soon as his left-wing began to fall apart. Attila also disengaged and turned back toward the fortified camp to avoid being surrounded. Sporadic combat persisted until dusk when it all stopped. Thorismund sought to besiege the Hunnic camp and continue the battle the following day after learning of his father's passing. But according to some traditions, Aetius mysteriously used his charm to warn the Visigothic heir apparent that it would be better for him to travel to Toulouse to claim his crown. Another legend claims that the Roman general was paid by the Hunnic monarch and may have sought to mend fences with the Huns so he could once more use their mercenaries to reassert his power in Gaul. Why Aetius didn't seize the initiative while he had Attila at his mercy is still a mystery. In all likelihood, though, he was forced to call off the battle after beating the Huns due to the inevitable dissolution of his temporary coalition.

Whatever the reason, Attila was able to leave the battlefield in good order and cross the Rhine to return. It is impossible to overstate Aetius' accomplishments on the Catalaunian fields. He was one of the greatest leaders of late antiquity thanks to his outstanding leadership, diplomatic, strategic, and tactical prowess in the defeat of the Huns. Attila, a former friend, was unable to establish a kingdom in Gaul but possessed great power and was unwilling to give up his plans to conquer the West. He invaded Italy the following year, shocking Aetius. Aquileia was surrounded and taken prisoner. The Po valley's cities were pillaged, but Ravenna, the region's capital, was shielded by the marshes that surrounded it. After moving further south, Attila abruptly withdrew because of a lack of supplies and a possible plague outbreak in his army.

He and his troops had already amassed a sizable amount of loot, and many of them were eager to return home before winter. Another justification for leaving Italy was the Eastern Empire's start of offensive operations against Attila's realm. Although Attila was not vanquished by Western Rome, his dominance depended on constant triumph, and the fact that he was unable to claim a decisive victory may have diminished his stature. Nevertheless, he intended to run again the next year. But in early 453, he married a young woman, and the next morning, after a night of excessive partying, he was discovered dead.

Although the precise reason for his death is unknown, the Hunnic empire fell apart within a few years as a result of the struggle for the succession between his sons and their numerous friends. Aetius also suffered the wrath of fate. Since he was no longer able to gather the Huns to fight for him, his authority started to dwindle. His military expertise was also less important once Attila was beaten. By 454, the general was aware of his perilous situation and wanted to use his clout with the emperor to maintain it by ensuring the union of his son and the emperor's daughter.

Although he was now in his 30s, Emperor Valentinian still hated Aetius. He was never able to rule independently, however, and was instead swayed by ambitious men in his court. Petronius Maximus, a senator who planned his ascent to power, was one such person. The senator convinced Valentinian to entice the general to a conference in Ravenna by taking advantage of his animosity for Aetius. Once there, Aetius was ambushed and killed by Valentinian and his eunuch chamberlain while they were having a conversation. Petronius, the provocateur, had bigger plans, though. A few months later, he enlisted the help of two of Aetius' bodyguards to kill Valentinian. Petronius soon proclaimed himself to be the next emperor. Within a few years of the war, all of the significant players in the circumstances surrounding the Catalaunian fields had passed away. In contrast, the Roman Empire would stutter along for a further 20 years.

Chapter *8*

Attila the Hun: The Scourge of God

He was a man created to terrify the earth, the bane of all places who in some manner horrified all of mankind due to the terrible rumors spread about him. Attila, who turned the Huns from a collection of nomadic tribes into an Empire that ruled the world with an unmatched speed and ferocity, is described in this way by modern historians. The Hunnic Empire is a suitable metaphor for the flame that burns twice as bright and burns half as long since they seemed to arise out of nowhere and almost soon became a power to be reckoned with, destroying all the nations that stood in their path. Even the Roman Empire came to fear Attila, whom they referred to as "The Scourge of God" or Flagellum Dei.

But after Attila passed away, the Hunnic Empire vanished as quickly as it had arisen. However, the Hunnic invasions led to a period of mass migrations in which Germanic tribes fled to the west to avoid the Huns' wrath, thus their influence was still felt. The Goths, the Vandals, the Lombards, the Franks, the Anglo-Saxons, and many more people traveled to other regions and lived there, leaving behind descendants who are still there today. Of course, the Romans already owned the majority of these regions and they were not about to relinquish them easily. The Western Roman Empire fell as a direct result of the conflicts between these two factions. It becomes clear that Attila's Hunnic invasions permanently altered the world's terrain.

The year of Attila's birth remains a significant open question. There have been dates put forth that span from the late fourth to the early fifth centuries AD. Some academics consider that 395 AD is the most plausible birth year for him, while others say that 406 AD is more likely based on the events in his life. Therefore, it can have been either the one or the other or something in between. The Huns, who were Attila's subjects, also experienced this ambiguity. They were a warrior nomadic people, thus there aren't many artifacts or cities that we can examine to learn about their civilization. When they decided to cross the Volga River and expand into Eastern and Central Europe towards the end of the 4th century, they merely "appeared" in the western historical record. Although historians have argued over their origins and even the languages they used, they have no definitive answers. One prevalent theory postulates a connection to an earlier nomadic group known as the Xiongnu and believed to have originated in Mongolia. They had been a part of the area since the third century BC and had fought the Chinese Han Dynasty for more than 200 years before being soundly defeated. However, this is mostly conjecture. Some contend that the Xiongnu were the Huns, while others think there was at least some continuity amongst the tribes. There are not many trustworthy sources available regarding Attila the person. Priscus of Panium, a Roman diplomat and historian who not only lived during the Hun's reign but also encountered Attila while on a diplomatic journey to his court, was a significant contribution.

Although Priscus's work did not survive on its whole, other historians like Jordanes and Cassiodorus referenced it, and as a result, we have portions of it in other texts that did survive. Priscus gives some information about Attila, including the following quote: "He was haughty in his walk, rolling his eyes hither and thither so that the might of his proud soul appeared in the movement of his body. He was a true lover of war, but he was restrained in his actions, wise in his advice, kind to suppliants, and forgiving to those who had formerly been under his protection. He had a huge head, a broad chest, and a low stature. His eyes were small, and he had a thin, gray beard. He also had a flat nose and a swarthy complexion, which were signs of his ancestry. Even though he had a naturally confident demeanor, the fact that Scythian rulers traditionally held the blade of Mars in the highest regard only strengthened his conviction.

The Huns had not yet come together as a single force when they initially arrived in Europe. They continued to be composed of loosely connected clans, each with its ruler. The Alans were their first significant target, and many other minors and obscure tribes that had the misfortune of being in their path were thereafter destroyed. Thervingi and Greuthungi were two Gothic nations that the Huns encountered as they invaded Europe. These, too, were unable to hold off the advancing hordes and had to flee even more to the west. Before they entered the Roman territory, it was only a matter of time.

By this time, the Roman Empire's dominance was waning. It used to rule over the majority of Europe as well as portions of Asia and Africa, but it was no longer the juggernaut it once was. It had been unofficially split into the Western and Eastern Roman Empires, giving rise to two political administrations, two emperors, and two capitals: the Eastern Roman Empire, also known as the Byzantine

Empire, had its center of power in Constantinople, while the Western Roman Empire no longer had Rome as its capital but instead had Mediolanum, or Milan. It should be noted that this separation between the east and west was made retroactively by modern scholars to make the two political units more clearly different.

At that time, Romans still thought of themselves as being merely citizens of a single Empire. The separation was also made with the advantage of hindsight because historians knew that the Byzantine Empire (another word used retroactively, by the way) would continue for another thousand years while the Western Roman Empire would entirely fall in the late 5th century. In any case, the Goths sought safety in the Roman Empire. They were initially allowed to settle by the Eastern Roman Emperor Valens, who probably saw them as a cheap army. However, the amount of land they were allocated was insufficient to accommodate all of the refugees from the Huns.

Due to a lack of food, there were uprisings and riots, which in 376 developed into a full-fledged war, one of many such confrontations between the Goths and the Romans. Naturally, during all of this, the Huns launched their assaults, attacking the Eastern Roman Empire's territories that corresponded to Western Asia, such as Cappadocia and Syria. They possibly likely attempted to take on the Sasanian or Neo-Persian Empire, but were unsuccessful and forced back into Europe. The Romans occasionally used the Huns as mercenaries to battle the Goths. One famous instance was the invasion of Italy by an Ostrogoth army under the command of King Radagaisus in 406 AD. To aid them in winning the war, the Romans hired Huns Alans, and other Goths as mercenaries. The Romans and the Huns maintained a tense partnership over the ensuing decades, but both sides occasionally ruptured it and engaged in hostilities. But something more significant took place.

A man by the name of Ruga, or Rugila occasionally, led the Huns to unify as a single force. He either governed alone as supreme monarch with the assistance of his brother Octar, or they shared leadership and each brother had control over half of their realm. In any case, Ruga was the only king of the Huns for a spell because Octar was the first to pass away, approximately 430 AD. Ruga also had a brother named Mundzuk, who had two sons named Bleda and Attila. When Ruga passed away in 434 AD, his two nephews took over as the new rulers of the Huns. We don't know if Ruga didn't have any offspring of his own or how the ascension process worked. Now in control of the Huns' territories, which were slowly expanding into a sizable Empire, were Bleda and Attila. Attila's Hunnic Empire equaled the Roman Empire in size by the time of his death.

We're not quite sure of the power relations between him and his brother. They likely had a system in place where each brother controlled half of the Empire, akin to Ruga and Octar.

However, it's also plausible that only one of them was considered the ultimate chieftain by the Huns. Whatever the connection was, it lasted for 11 years, up until Bleda's passing in the year 445 AD. Although the traditional texts indicate that Attila killed his brother to seize sole control of the Huns, it shouldn't come as a surprise to learn that those circumstances are likewise rather ambiguous. We now move to Priscus, who claimed that "the intrigues of his brother Attila resulted in the assassination of Bleda, king of the Huns."

However, we're getting a little ahead of ourselves, so let's start with Attila's accession to the throne. The Romans were the first problem that needed to be resolved. Rome's attitude toward the Huns at the time was largely neutral, but they had to take into account the possibility that Ruga's nephews might have different plans. The Romans already paid tribute to the Huns, and it turned out that they would be willing to pay even more in exchange for peace. The Treaty of Margus, which was largely in the Huns' favor, was signed by the two parties in 435. They would receive a fixed annual tribute from the Roman Empire of 700 pounds of gold, which was twice as much as before. They also swore to repatriate Hunnic refugees and refrain from forging friendships with Hunnish foes. Attila thought this was a very good offer, so he put off his desire to fight the Romans for the time being. He instead decided to invade Persia once more and attempt to overthrow the Sasanian Empire, hoping to triumph where his forerunners had failed.

Since the Romans were not involved, we don't have reliable evidence for this period of his reign, but suffice it to state that Attila was beaten and had to flee back to Europe. The King of Burgundy, Gundahar, was his first aim there. The king, sometimes known as Gunther or Gunnar, made his way into many folklore tales and may be found in both the Germanic Song of the Nibelungs and the Nordic Poetic Edda. Attila himself killed King Gundahar in battle in 437, according to mythology. It is much less likely for the historical one. The Burgundians' main adversaries were the Romans, while the Huns were subordinate mercenaries under the terms of their pact. The province of Belgica Prima had been overrun by the Burgundians after they had entered Roman Gaul. Naturally, the Romans retaliated, and with the aid of the Huns, they vanquished their adversary in combat.

They then kept up their assault and overran the Kingdom of Burgundy. During the latter years of the Western Roman Empire, Flavius Aetius, a strong and prominent commander,

94

was in charge of the army. He earned the moniker "Last of the Romans" as a result, and according to historian Edward Gibbon, he was "universally praised as the dread of the Barbarians and the support of the republic." Because he will have a more significant role later, we are highlighting him now. Everyone understood that the two powers' peace accord would not last for long. Moesia and Illyricum were pillaged by the Huns as they invaded the Eastern Roman Empire in 441 by crossing the Danube. The Treaty of Margus was terminated as a result, but the Huns insisted that the Romans were the ones to break it first. We are unable to determine if this was real or if it was just a pretext for theft and looting.

The Huns attacked just after Roman Emperor Theodosius II moved the garrisons guarding that border to dispatch them to battle the Vandals in Africa, which raised some questions about the date of the attack. The most plausible explanation was that Attila merely identified a weakness and chose to take advantage of it. He was very prosperous in that way. Several Roman cities were pillaged by the Huns, and some were almost destroyed. By 443, Theodosius was prepared to ratify a new pact that would be even more advantageous to the Huns. Attila was satiated by this and once more withdrew into the core of his Empire. Some historians contend that there may have been an unrecorded emergency that required

Attila's attention; otherwise, he would not have had a motive to halt the invasion given the obvious superiority of his army. At this time, Bleda also passed away, making Attila the only Hun chieftain. We can only hazard a guess as to how the two might be related. It is unknown if the Romans truly paid their tribute. They most likely simply paused for a few years while attempting to fortify their defenses in preparation for the inevitable day when the Huns came once more. This occurred in 447 when Attila reentered the Eastern Roman Empire with his army and decimated every province in the Balkan region.

According to a source from the time, the Huns conquered more than a hundred cities before turning around and retreating to Thermopylae in Greece. These may have been necessary sacrifices because the Romans concluded that they needed to combine all of their forces into one strong army rather than letting them wither away slowly while defending each city. The Battle of the Utus in Dacia, Ripensis, close to the present-day river Vit in Bulgaria, marked the end of the invasion. Arnegisclus, who held the title of magister militum—at the time, the highest military rank in the Empire—led the Romans. The Romans were vanquished by the Huns, but not before Arnegisclus perished in battle, and many Romans were seriously hurt. After that, Attila had his sights set on Constantinople, the imperial seat of the Eastern Roman Empire—the greatest prize imaginable.

Attila, however, was not powerful enough to capture the city due to the renowned Walls of Constantinople, Roman reinforcements traveling from Asia Minor, as well as all the losses the Huns suffered in the Battle of the Utus. He was aware of this, therefore he did not attempt.

Instead, he ratified a fresh peace accord. This time, Attila received a tribute that was triple what it had been previously: 2,100 pounds of gold annually along with a lot of additional perks.

The Huns retired to the Great Hungarian Plains after one battle was over, but they only stayed there long enough to build up their numbers and strength before setting out again for battle. They set out once more in 450, but they chose not to attack the Eastern Roman Empire this time. Attila instead concentrated on its western equivalent. This choice was a little unexpected. Did Attila no longer desire to take Constantinople? That same year, Theodosius passed away, and Marcian succeeded him as emperor. Formerly a general, the latter dealt with the Huns in a very different way, instantly terminating their treaty and stopping all payments. This would have provided Attila with the perfect excuse—not that he needed one—to launch another assault on the

Eastern Roman Empire, but he stuck to his original plans to invade the west. Attila wanted to go that way because he planned to fight the Visigoths as well as the Romans, the historian Jordanes claims. Gaiseric, King of the Vandals, who lavished the commander of the Huns with gifts and incited him against Theodoric, King of the Visigoths for his vengeance, may or may not have asked him to do this. Attila gave a bizarre and unusual explanation for why he invaded the Western Roman Empire. Valentinian III served as the western emperor. Honoria, one of his sisters, was set to wed Bassus Herculanus, a senator. Honoria's brother had set up the marriage, but she didn't want to go through with it, so she turned to Attila the Hun for assistance by sending him a letter and a ring.

Honoria left a note that we don't know what was written or what type of assistance she anticipated, but Attila opted to read it as a proposal of marriage. In addition, he believed he was entitled to receive as dowry half of the Western Roman Empire. Attila would arrive to reclaim what was rightfully his, and he even dispatched a messenger to Valentinian to affirm that the proposition had been real. It's unlikely that Attila genuinely cared about the union or thought the Roman emperor would just hand over half of his Empire. Most likely, he was using this as yet another handy pretext to start a conflict. Attila occupied Roman Gaul in 451. Jordanes claimed to have a half-million-man army, although contemporary historians estimate it to be closer to 200,000. In either case, it was a powerful force that swiftly wiped out everybody who got in its way. Cities like Trier and Metz were virtual without resistance taken over and pillaged.

Do you remember the proverb, "My enemy is my friend"? That is how the Romans felt as well, as seen by Valentinian's call for assistance from the local Gothic groups, who, but for the Huns, most likely would have been at war with the Roman Empire. "Bravest of nations, it is wise for us to join against the lord of the earth who seeks to subjugate the entire world; who requires no just cause for battle but assumes that all he does is right," he wrote in an embassy. He gauges his ambition based on his power. His pride is sated by his license. He reveals himself to be an adversary of Nature herself by scorning law and right. And as a result, everyone should hate the person who is undeniably their shared enemy. Realizing that they were in equal danger from the Huns as the Romans were, the Franks, the Saxons, the Burgundians, the Alans, and particularly the Visigoths led by King Theodoric decided to create an alliance to battle Attila and his army.

Flavius Aetius, a commander who had previously fought alongside the Romans against the Burgundians, led the charge against the Huns. On June 20, 451 AD, he led a coalition of nations against the Huns in the Battle of Châlons, also referred to as the Battle of the Catalaunian Fields. Witnesses stated that thousands of bodies were piling up on the plains, making it one of the bloodiest military confrontations in history up to that moment. They further claimed that Attila had built a sizable funeral pyre inside the Hunni camp and was preparing to jump on it and burn alive rather than be captured.

Most historians think that the Romans and the Visigoths won the fight, although suffering significant losses. Historians have varying viewpoints on the outcome of this conflict and its historical significance. King Theodoric was killed in battle, and his son Thorismund wished to enter the Huns' camp and exterminate them permanently. If Aetius hadn't intervened on behalf of Attila and persuaded the young Thorismund that, as the new King of the Visigoths, he ought to return to their city of Toulouse and cement his position against his conspiring siblings, they might have been able to pull it off as well. Why would Aetius act in such a way when he had the chance to get rid of the Huns? He did so out of concern that the Visigoths might develop into an even more deadly adversary and one that was much closer to his frontiers.

As long as Attila existed, he functioned as a helpful ally who brought the Romans and the Goths together. Attila was able to flee and live to fight another day as a result. He did fight because less than a year had elapsed when the Huns attacked the Western Roman Empire once more. This time, they entered Italy right away with the clear intention of plundering the most important Roman cities.

The worst of it was almost destroyed in the city of Aquileia. The Huns next advanced into the province of Venetia, where they destroyed more towns. Tradition holds that this resulted in the establishment of the city of Venice. It was founded by refugees who fled other towns to avoid the Huns, and they were right to assume that Attila's horsemen would not pursue them into the lagoon that surrounds Venice. The Romans could not stop Attila without the help of the Gothics.

Pope Leo, I was one of many envoys that the emperor ultimately dispatched to the Huns to broker a peace treaty. According to accounts from the time, Leo is credited for persuading Attila to turn around after impressing him with his words and piety. Although the specifics of their encounter are unknown, contemporary historians offer more plausible explanations for Attila's retreat, including a lack of food due to a famine, a disease that spread among his soldiers, and the fact that an army from the Eastern Roman Empire crossed the Danube and launched a counterattack on Hunnic settlements. Whatever the motivation, Attila would have invaded again if given the chance.

However, his life abruptly ended in 453 AD while he was toasting the nuptials of his new bride, Ildikó. The chief of the Huns choked on his blood, either from a burst blood vessel or a particularly strong nosebleed, according to the ancient historian Priscus, who claimed that the leader of the Huns had fallen on his bed in a drunken stupor with his head leaned back.

Alternative theories include Ildikó killing him or Attila passing away from an internal hemorrhage brought on by overdrinking. All of the Hun soldiers shaved off their long hair and cut their cheeks as a sign of mourning, "so that the greatest of all warriors might be mourned not with tears or the crying of women, but with the blood of men," according to the legend.

Their customs stressed how crucial it was for the chieftain's final resting site to remain unknown. Since Attila was the greatest leader they had ever known, he was interred in three different caskets: a gold casket, a silver casket, and an iron casket. To ensure that no one was still alive who knew the location of Attila the Hun's last burial place, the coffin was then buried in a riverbed, and those who did it were afterward slain.

Chapter 9

The Man Who Broke Rome

In Nicest in 443 AD, a scene that had just come from the end of the world was taking place. The only survivors of a violent siege and massacre that saw the town razed and its inhabitants slaughtered in the middle of haunting singing and chanting were a small handful of monks. It must have appeared like the end of the world among the rubble. This chapter will explain how the self-styled Scourge of God, or Attila the Hun as history called him, decimated this city as well as numerous others.

One of the many Balkan cities the Huns destroyed was Nicest in modern-day Serbia, but the history of this war begins decades earlier, more than 1,000 miles away, on the steps of Kazakhstan, which is thought to have been the Huns' native homeland. One of the primary causes of the fall of the Roman

Empire was the Huns' decision to move in large numbers into Europe. Massive human waves from various tribes like the Goths, Burgundians, Lombardians, and Vandals were driven into the Roman Empire by this large-scale financial movement. Many of them were frantically trying to find safety as these enormous waves of refugees flooded in. At the Battle of Edrine Opal in 375 AD, Rome's army was so weak that it was powerless to stop the incursions, many of whom had violent intents to attempt to suppress this. Some took up weapons and fought their way in. The Romans employed mercenaries from the Hun nation, such as Ruga, who commanded his troops in a brutal campaign in France against the Goth invaders.

The Huns and Romans would meet for the first time at this point, and the campaign would teach them two lessons. First, the Roman Empire had a lot of wealth to loot, and second, it was in such need of labor. When troops were occupied, they could be easily attacked and taken advantage of. Later, Ruga, the Hun chief, passed away and was succeeded by his infamous nephew Attila. A shepherd child is said to have given Attila a mystical sword that was blazing and stuck in the ground when he was out on the steps.

Attila announced that he had been sent to scourge the newly converted Romans with the blade of Mars, the Roman God of War. Attila is thought to have come from a well-respected

Hun clan, and unlike European leaders who took the throne after their fathers, clans like the Huns allowed whoever showed the power to rule to do so.

Attila killed his cousins and, subsequently, his older brother Bleda to show off his might as the unchallenged king of the Huns. He would lead a violent uprising that would bring the Roman Empire to its absolute breaking point. Vandals in North Africa were posing a danger to taking control of the Roman port of Carthage and the nearby productive agricultural land in 439 AD. This would be Attila's chance, due to conflict on the other side of the slowly disintegrating Roman Empire and a little bit of false flag action.

The Romans deployed troops to Sicily to combat them because they could not simply let things happen. Attila had a remarkable sense of timing and struck while the Roman army was dispersed. The Roman cities of the Balkans were accessible from Africa, but he required a false flag to support his attack. Attila's men embarrassed the Romans by refusing to dismount their horses during negotiations at the city of Margam, which served as the frontier between the eastern Roman Empire and the Huns. Instead, before any negotiations could begin, the Romans had to mount their horses. Attila falsely claimed that a Christian Bishop had stolen treasure from Hun graves, breaking a peace agreement they had already signed. A bishop was committing late-night grave robbing, which served as the pretext for a disastrous campaign. The city of Margam, which had no defensive forces because they had been deployed, was then destroyed by Attila.

In Africa, the Huns were feared for their bows and arrows and were known for their cavalry combat, which allowed them to travel great distances swiftly. Numerous cities, including Sophia, Belgrade, and Plovdiv, were attacked in large numbers by Hun raids. Attila's crusade had accomplished three goals in a ruthless terror campaign. First of all, it had made gaps all along the eastern Roman Empire's border, leaving it open to further assault. Second, by giving Attila's lieutenants a share of the enormous sums of wealth looted from these cities, the Luton could maintain his position by benefiting allies. In the end, it coerced the Romans into ratifying a peace accord. Through this agreement, Attila received an annual transfer of gold equal to 3% of the riches of the Roman Empire in exchange for his promise not to wage war. To prevent other ambitious chiefs from stealing money, he also ordered that all payments be transferred directly to him. However, a few years later, his appetite was piqued once more—this time, it wasn't through politics or false flags, but rather a very real intervention from nature.

A significant earthquake that struck Constantinople in 447 AD caused the city's walls to collapse, opening the city up to attack. Emperor Theodosius wailed, prayed, and begged God to save the city as he walked barefoot through the metropolis. In the interim, the populace labored nonstop to try and restore the walls. The inhabitants were racing the Hun forces that had heard of the earthquake and were advancing south. Only recently recuperating from their previous campaign, the Huns once more participated in widespread plundering, raping, and murder in several places. As it turned out, there was just enough time to rebuild the walls.

The fact that the Hun war carts were now so loaded down with warlords that their army was traveling more slowly was one factor that helped them. Given that the city's defenses had been restored and that the Huns had sent Edeko as their ambassador to request a new treaty, Attila decided against attacking the city. After being entertained and fed, Edeko was promised a sizable payoff if he could assassinate Attila. Edeko concurred, and Rome now needed a pretext to approach Attila. That pretext was a diplomatic journey to his court outside the Danube.

The tiny company of Romans and their Hun guide wound their way through the Balkans as Edeko served as their guide. Nothing but burned-out farms, destroyed cities, and bleached skeletons could be seen along the journey. The

Roman delegation, who were on their route to a meeting, must have found it unsettling to be reminded of the man's terrible potential. They eventually arrived at Attila's court, a huge tent encircled by Hun war wagons and a few smaller tents. Priskus, a Roman guest, wrote a description of the meal that Attila hosted for his visiting Roman guests. He provides the most thorough portrayal of Attila's personality and the Huns' organizational structure. He notes that Huns flattened faces by strapping boards on the faces of their infants to flatten them. The Romans would have found them uncomfortable in appearance because of this; in fact, this tale is the only source for Attila's existence and only physical description.

Attila's beard is characterized as being slightly gray and having a black tone. He also has a huge head, a broad torso, and small eyes. As the feast progressed, the Romans observed that, in contrast to the majority of the visitors, Attila himself was satisfied to eat from a plain wooden board. He did not chuckle at any of the entertainment for the evening, and his only tenderness came when he hugged his young son Ernakh. A leader who showed this level of restraint and thrift when attending banquets was well-liked in the Roman culture. The Romans visited Attila once more the following day and sent their best wishes to him via his interpreter. Attila replied coolly that he wished the Roman emperor all the best because he now knew that the emperor wanted to keep him hidden from the Roman envoy. Attila discovered the conspiracy against him, but instead of responding immediately, he thought he might use this to his advantage. He would permit the Romans to get the gold from Constantinople and return to the Danube to pay the murderer. Like his false flag story about the Bishop, they might be searched once they got back and the gold recovered. He was skilled at planting evidence and setting up traps to further his own goals. Although Attila was far from a thug and was instead a brilliant and calculated strategist, another wave of mob action began what can only be characterized as a love letter as earthquakes and combat scenes from the end times filled his existence. Attila was once more visited by Romans in 450 AD, although this time there was only one Eunuch and no diplomatic delegation.

Eunuchs' exceptionally high voices from being castrated as boys would have initially alarmed Attila. Nevertheless, this Eunuch made a powerful offer. The lute, which the Hun war commander was unable to reject, included a young woman by the name of Inoria who had dispatched the Eunuch. The sister of the western Roman emperor Valentinian was on this unlawful mission on Orio, and he wished to marry her off to a strong man because she had lost her virginity. She could not be wed off to a strong foreign monarch as a virgin in a palace romance with a lowly servant. She was furious when Emperor Valentinian made her marry a merchant and made the decision to take action. To establish that the letter was written by her, she sent an expensive ring to Attila's lands along with a note requesting him to come and liberate her from the marriage. Attila decided to move after spotting the ring, but romance was the last thing on his mind. The Western Romans received word from Attila that he would be arriving to claim Minori as one of his many wives. He also insisted she is given control of the Western Roman Empire. He would effectively become the western Roman emperor by demanding that. Emperor Valentinian was unable to accept the action.

When his mother intervened, Valentinian threatened to deport his sister, claiming that doing so may be interpreted as a sign of weakness. Instead, she was married off to the merchant and spent the rest of her life in the isolated Italian countryside, but Attila was now on the move. While he was at it, Attila threatened the newly installed martian emperor of the Eastern Roman Empire to gauge his adherence to the peace accord. Princess Honorio had informed the Eastern Emperor of Attila's interest, and since she felt he was concentrating on the West, she scoffed at domestic threats. As the Huns advanced toward the west, Attila decided to continually threaten Western Emperor Valentinian. Attila is your lord and your lord has ordered you to prepare the palace for him, the Hun ambassador remarked to Valentinian as he entered the Roman palace. However, unlike many of the things Attila did, this threat was not made in a vulgar manner by the Hun warlord through his ambassador; rather, it was based on sound strategic reasoning. Attila personally threatened the Emperor to persuade him to keep his forces in Italy for his security.

This would imply that the goths would be the only group defending Attila's true aim, France. Attila was sure he could defeat both the Goths and the Romans, but not if they collaborated. He used threats against the Emperor to get him to leave his men in Italy so he could defend himself, leaving the Goths to defend themselves against the Hun horde by themselves. Attila's campaign in France was brutal, and Western Christians would experience the apocalypse just as the monks of the eastern Empire had interpreted the Huns as a sign of the end of the world. According to local lore, the apostles appeared in the skies and consented to the city's attack as a punishment for its crimes, therefore the city of Mets was pillaged. When a Hun raider charged into the church and beheaded the priest, the priest's mouth continued to recite Psalm 119. The profoundly superstitious Huns were so alarmed by this that they withdrew to Orleans, a city not far from where Joan of Arc would be born centuries later. Lookouts atop the city cathedral tower noticed a dust cloud in the distance as the Huns pounded on the city gates. A Roman army was sent to unite with the neighborhood Goths and face Attila as the "dust cloud." Attila made a serious mistake in assuming the Romans would risk everything to keep their hold on France, even if it meant leaving the Emperor in Italy defenseless. At this point, decisions were typically decided by Roman generals rather than emperors. Attila believed in the absolute control of his people, therefore the thought that a ruler could be overridden by generals was inconceivable. This may help to explain why he made such a grave error in judgment when the Roman generals decided to leave the Emperor undefended while they went to battle for France. A Roman emperor might be readily overthrown by harsh contrast, even while Western Emperor Valentinian was personally in danger. If France fell into Hun's hands, it would not be as readily replaced as Julius Caesar's costly conquest of the country years earlier.

As a result, Attila's worry about having to deal with many forces materialized. The Battle of the Catalonian Fields—not to be confused with Catalonia in Spain—was fought in the champagne region between the Roman army and their French Catholic allies against Attila. The Huns suffered surprisingly high casualties in this fierce battle. At one point, the Huns retreated behind their row of wagons, and Attila ordered a stack of saddles to be built. At that point, Attila roared that he might soon be taken alive. He would jump into the burning saddles and be burned to death rather than being captured by the Romans. The combat then went on with additional significant casualties. The Goths started to retire the next day, and Attila initially believed this was a ruse to pull his men into open terrain. However, it soon became evident that this was the case. Did he allow his soldiers to retreat? Attila gambled that the Romans would not come and aid the Goths in France because they had the victories and loot, he had promised his men had materialized no Hun chief could ever survive if he was seen to have withdrawn in defeat, so he launched an attack on a nearly defenseless Italy to salvage his reputation. The forces that had been dispatched to meet him in France had been withdrawn from Italy. The Huns were supposed to need at least a few months to recover before conquering Italy, thus the Romans were severely caught off guard by this surprise attack that occurred soon after the Hun losses.

In Qualia, the once-bustling harbor was burnt and pillaged, and the survivors fled across the lagoon to build the current city of Venice. Similar to what had happened at Pompey, a layer of ash fell over the church mosaics as a result of the looting and fire, magnificently preserving them. At this point, the Roman Emperor was located in Ravina, although Rome was still a major target for Attila. I don't know what happened after that. Most likely, someone sent a request for negotiations with Attila from outside the city. After some period of conversation between the two men, Attila's army abruptly left. A more plausible explanation is that Attila's forces were at the very end of their supply lines due to crop failures over the years, which meant that there was significantly less food to plunder in the Italian countryside. According to legend, Saint Peter and Saint Paul had appeared beside the pope and scared Attila away. More than Attila had anticipated, his army required food, which Italy itself was unable to supply. Attila learned that the Eastern Roman Emperor had dispatched an expeditionary force over the Danube to exact revenge on the local Hun population. With more important issues at hand, Attila hurried back and decided that a protracted siege of Rome was not worth it. Attila's violent and spiteful approach to his Hun army is reported to have kept the Eastern Roman Emperor Martian up for days.

But according to legend, an angel once descended to the emperor's deathbed and smashed a bow and arrow. He received the word that Attila had died the next morning, which was a sign that an enemy was likely to be vanquished. Instead of dying on the battlefield, he suffocated to death while intoxicated and choking on a nosebleed. Without the charisma, strength, and ruthlessness of their famous warlord, the Huns quickly started to fall apart. His sons fought among themselves for dominance. Ernak, one of the sons, decided to leave Europe and vanished from history. Den Gizich, one of the brothers, rejected his sibling as a coward and fought the Eastern Roman Empire. He lost the struggle and had his head severed. While Attila was dead and its soldiers were gone, the damage they inflicted by roaming had a significant impact on its existence. His skull was paraded through the streets to the applause of the public before being hanged on the city walls of Constantinople to decay. Numerous diverse tribes had been driven over the Roman frontier by the Huns' raids across Europe. These tribes settled down and were content to employ force to maintain their position.

Due to the Empire's incapacity to control these tribes and their ongoing territorial ambitions, both the Empire as a whole and Rome's internal authority were severely damaged. A short time after Attila's passing, Vandals and Goths, who had both originally been forced into the Empire by the Huns, outdid the Huns and both sacked Rome. The last Roman emperor quickly became so unimportant that he was simply pensioned off and banished to the countryside. Attila the Hun may have done more than any other man to bring down

the splendor that was his reign, but even though the hun menace only lasted a few decades, it had a terrible effect on the Roman Empire.

Chapter *10*

Unsettling Huns and Attila Facts

The Roman Empire was experiencing its final years as a powerful force on the continent as Europe progressively moved from the Classical Era to more medieval times. At least the western half. The Byzantine Empire lasted in the east until the fifteenth century. In any case, the Western Roman Empire collapsed largely as a result of the numerous internal power conflicts as well as the numerous barbaric assaults from Central and Eastern Europe.

However, as the Romans would soon discover, these barbarous tribes were fleeing a menace like never before: the Huns, rather than seeking loot or conquests. The Huns invaded Europe with a suddenness and fury never before witnessed on the "Old Continent," and for a short time—not even a century—they would cause so much carnage and havoc that it would permanently cement their position in history.

Shaping a baby's head

The technique of "artificial cranial deformation," often known as "baby head shaping," is almost as old as humanity itself. The practice was carried out all over the world, including in various regions of Europe and Africa as well as Asia, the Americas, Oceania, and Africa. In France, cranial deformation was used well into the 19th century. Although in no way risky, the process does alter one's physical look. From place to area, different methods are employed, such as employing cloth or wooden planks to obtain the desired effect.

Around the world, flat, elongated, rounded, and conical cranial forms were among the most desired. A baby's skull is extremely pliable between the ages of one and six months, and during this time, its head is firmly wrapped in cotton to give it an alien-looking head shape. Archaeological evidence suggests that head sculpting was also a technique among the Huns. The many peoples of Europe, notably the Romans, thought the Huns were completely absurd due to their ethnic roots. This fact is supported by numerous contemporary descriptions. Understandably, the people the Huns assaulted and massacred thought the Huns had weird-shaped heads. In actuality, the Huns were responsible for introducing the custom to the European nations they conquered, including the French stated earlier.

Their male children were scarred by the Huns.

While the "head shaping" indicated above was probably done for aesthetic reasons or even to distinguish between the classes, the scarring they inflicted on their male infants had a very other function. Male babies were made to undergo anguish on the day of their birth by being sliced with a sword on both cheeks.

A Gothic historian named Jordanes, who resided in a province on the Lower Danube during the Byzantine Empire's 6th century AD, had the following to say about this Hunnic custom: "For by the terror of their features they instilled great fear in people whom perhaps they did not truly surpass in fighting. They frightened their enemies with their swarthy faces, making them run in horror. Their wild appearance makes their stoicism clear, and they are creatures who are brutal to their offspring from the moment they are born. Because they use a sword to slash the males' cheeks, they are forced to become wound-tolerant before they can consume milk. Anyone who heard him speak on the battlefield must have felt the truth of what he said. The Huns were fighting a psychological battle with their foes in addition to their visibly different head shape, temperament, and ruthless character. Another Roman historian, Ammianus Marcellinus, stated the following about the practice: "At the very moment of their birth, the cheeks of their infant offspring are profoundly scarred by an iron."

The Paleo/Hunnic Diet

The Huns' favored foods are also described by the historian Marcellinus, who previously mentioned. And even though they only hideously resemble men, their level of civilization is so low that they do not employ fire or any other form of relish in the preparation of their food instead subsisting on the roots they find in the fields and the half-raw meat of any kind of animal. These remarks reflect the Romans' animosity toward the invading barbarians. However, it appears that this tale has some connection to actual events. Similar to their nomadic successors, the Huns of the fifth century were cooking their meals in a similar way to the Mongols who plagued Europe some 750 years later. They spent the majority of the day riding while mounted, sandwiching some wrapped pork between the horse and their saddle.

The meat would grow more tender due to the constant pressure and pounding of riding and combined with the salt from the horse's back, the Hunnic delicacy would also gain a coating of preservative and a little flavor. In other words, the Huns were consuming salted jerky that had been produced between a rock and a particularly hard Hunnic rock. However, it doesn't sound so horrible when contrasted with the maggoty cheese produced in Sardinia, Italy, does it?

Hunnic War Machine

Scholars continue to discuss whether or not the previously powerful Xiongnu people, also known as the Hsiung-nu, were the forefathers of the Huns. Some people think they were the forerunners of modern Turks. or perhaps both. However, the Xiongnu certainly forced the Chinese to the south to be forced to construct their massive wall in the first place. The Hsiung-nu originated in the Central Asian steppes, just like the Huns. As many of us already know, this area of the planet was ideal for raising mounted warriors. The Hsiung-nu and the Huns were so powerful and successful against the Chinese and the early Christians, respectively, because they rode horses. In any case, confronting an army largely composed of infantry, fighting only on horseback offered a significant advantage. The Huns lived a nomadic life, appearing to the Europeans as though they were practically attached to their saddles. They were said to do practically everything from atop their horses, including eating, sleeping, and even bartering.

As soon as they could walk, the Huns were taught how to ride a horse and, from the top of their mount, how to use a bow. A technical achievement of the fifth century was the Hunnic bow. Being a reflex bow, it bent back on itself as it was strung, giving it more tension than any other bow at the time. A warrior could shoot an arrow three times that distance and kill a man at a distance of 80 yards. The saddle was another crucial distinction between the Huns and their adversaries in terms of fighting. The Hun saddles had a high front and back part, in contrast to other saddles used by the Romans and other Europeans. These provided the rider with incredible stability, making him feel virtually fixed to his horse. In this manner, he could turn 360 degrees without the danger of falling off while firing his long-range bow in all directions. The lasso was a common weapon in battle among the Huns. Typically, they would fight and travel in groups of little more than a few hundred riders. If they came across an adversary, they would charge in and launch a lightning-fast attack from atop their horses, escape, and then emerge somewhere else to launch another attack. Naturally, this doesn't imply that they didn't frequently gather together in bigger numbers, as they frequently did. They would be able to quickly erect a fort if they were ever ambushed by surprise by simply enclosing their wagons in a circle.

Attila the God-Hateful

Attila the Hun was a member of the most affluent family north of the Danube when he was born somewhere in the first century AD.

Two of Attila's uncles, Octar and Rugila, governed the Huns while he was a child. Both Attila and his elder brother Bleda received the Hunnish throne from their uncles in the year 434 AD. A sort of peace contract between themselves and the Byzantine Empire was their first order of business. In exchange for the Huns not attacking the Empire, the Romans were required to pay 700 pounds of gold every year under the terms of this contract. After a few years, Attila claimed that the Byzantines were not making their payments and launched a series of destructive assaults across the Eastern Empire. Emperor Theodosius was forced to pay Attila 2,100 pounds of gold annually to make him leave despite being only about 20 miles from Constantinople.

Then, in 445 AD, Attila's brother perplexingly passed away. Some claim that Attila killed his brother to seize total power over the Huns. Whatever the reason, he did seize power, and for the entirety of the Hunnic Kingdom's existence, he was the only one in charge. Attila conducted numerous military expeditions throughout the Balkans, Greece, Italy, Gaul, and the Baltics during his reign, leaving nothing but death and destruction in his wake. He had no desire to rule or conquest any of the people he had vanquished. Attila's primary objective was to plunder and pillage, grabbing anything he could. He would be considered a terrorist in every sense of the term today since fear was one of his strongest weapons. He earned the moniker "the Scourge of God" as a result of this. Most of the information we have about him indeed comes from his adversaries, and at best, these portrayals can be characterized as subjective. But both his behavior and his approach to fighting seem to point in the same direction.

Nevertheless, he is shown to be honest, modest, and considerate of emissaries. In 453 AD, on the eve of his wedding, he passed away in bed. His sons received equal shares of the kingdom after his death, but as soon as they started warring, the Huns vanished from history.

The Huns and the Germanic Tribes to the East The Huns arrived in southern Russia in the fourth century AD after traveling steadily west from Central Asia. The Goths lived here, but it was also a country of lush pastures and grasslands. These were members of the Germanic tribes known as the Visigoths (to the west) and Ostrogoths, which later broke apart (to the east). These people were the first to experience the Huns' dreadful power when they arrived in Eastern Europe. The Ostrogoths were repeatedly massacred by the Huns, who suddenly appeared out of nowhere; almost anyone survived to tell the tale. The Visigoths, who were the most fortunate to be able to retreat, entered Byzantine territory south of the Danube River. Ermanaric, the Ostrogothic king, killed himself as the Huns invaded his realm. The remaining Ostrogoths who couldn't flee were ruled by the Huns for the next 75 years. They later joined the Huns in battle during many of their conquests, frequently serving as foot troops. After several abortive uprisings, they finally succeeded in escaping the brutal Huns only after Attila's demise. Theodimir, the leader of the Ostrogoths, and their former adversaries, the Gepids, were able to defeat the Huns at the Battle of Nedao in 454 and restore their freedom.

The Burgundy Slaughter

The initial encounters between the Huns and the Romans went more smoothly than was anticipated. In reality, the Romans hired the Huns as mercenaries and assassins to fight for them instead of engaging in open combat. Given the Romans' affluence at the time and their recognition of the Huns' military prowess, Attila was unable to ignore their offer. The Romans promised the Huns vast riches in exchange for their allegiance. In what is now France, in the year 437 AD, the Huns mounted a massive assault on the Burgundians.

The Western Roman Empire, at least in its later years, was reluctant to use its legions for waging war outside of its borders out of fear of a civil war. Numerous savage tribes, including the Burgundians, profited from the situation as the Emperors gradually lost control over the integrity of the Empire. The Huns were used by the Roman general Aetius against the Romans because of their frequent invasions of Roman territory. They all give slightly different stories of what happened next, but one thing is for sure: the Kingdom of Burgundy was destroyed. It appears that Aetius attacked them in 436 and was successful in doing so. King Gundahar of Burgundy and Aetius agreed to a peace deal. The Huns would destroy the Burgundian's "root and branch" little more than a year after this brief period of peace. The peace deal probably caught the Hunnic onslaught off guard, which led to the horror. According to historical accounts, Attila first killed the defenders before turning on the women and children. An epic-scale ethnic cleansing claimed the lives of an estimated 20,000 people. In the conflict, King Gundahar was killed, and the Burgundian First Kingdom fell. The goal of this raid was to terrorize all adversaries of the Huns and to plunder as much as possible, not to conquer and subjugate other peoples.

Taking Naissus Prisoner in Modern-Day Serbia

The Huns were a nomadic people that lived largely off of pillage and plunder. Attila was aware that he would have to give his troops a steady stream of gold to maintain their devotion. He would have to focus on the Roman Empire itself to do this, setting his sights on considerably greater goals than he had before. He had to demonstrate that he would become a significant issue and a menace if the Romans refused to pay up to extract money from them. Finding a Roman city and destroying it was the best way to accomplish this. The present city of Naissus resembles a castle more than anything else. His intended victim was Ni in Serbia, which was then a part of the Byzantine Empire. Naissus, which was the birthplace of numerous Roman emperors, including Constantine the Great, came under Hunnid assault in 441 AD.

The Huns weren't well suited to capturing a heavily guarded castle, however, as they fought mostly on horseback, and Attila's initial wave of mounted men was easily beaten back. The battering ram, one of the most basic siege engines, helped the Huns overcome this obstacle, though. But in addition to them, the Huns also employed certain siege towers and climbing ladders. The Huns finally succeeded in breaching the city's fortifications by simultaneously attacking various points of the wall with their crude siege engines. Naissus served as a major regional trading center and trove of riches, but it was also a Byzantine army's weapons manufacturing. Attila brought all the experienced laborers he could find along with him in addition to the gold and supplies found within. He burned the city down after massacring the remaining residents. Naissus was still in ruins and uninhabited when the Greek diplomat and historian Priscus of Panium visited it several years later, except for a few sick persons receiving care inside the church.

The Extortion Ring Run by a Mob and the Cruel Punishments

Attila used psychological warfare based on fear as his primary method of attack, similar to other terrorists both past and present.

Long before he did, his horrifying massacres and heinous murders had reached Constantinople. The news that he had managed to seize control of a heavily fortified Roman city and kill everyone inside undoubtedly terrified the people of Constantinople to the hilt. Additionally, on November 6, 447, a strong earthquake severely damaged a huge portion of the city's defenses, leaving them completely open to attack by Attila and his Huns. Fortunately, Emperor Theodosius II assigned Kyros of Floros, an urban prefect, to supervise the restoration of Constantinople's defenses. He was able to not only repair the damaged portions of the wall in under 60 days, but he also added an outer wall, a moat, and other improvements. And it couldn't have come at a better time since Attila was moving in their direction.

However, the citizens of the city were so terrified of his reputation that they ignored their strong defenses, which Attila was completely unprepared to conquer. As a result, the Emperor was forced to bribe the Huns with a stunning 6,000 pounds of gold (approximately $100 million) to get them to leave. Additionally, Attila sought the return of his deserters who had deserted the camp and were now living in Constantinople. Of course, the Byzantines were happy to comply with his request and return the deserters. They were all impaled as a kind of retribution for their disloyalty, and they endured a grisly death while hanging from spikes for as long as two days before dying.

The Catalaunian Plains Battle and Attila's Subsequent Retaliation

Attila understood there wouldn't be any more significant riches to be obtained in the Eastern Empire once he had successfully extracted practically every single euro from its coffers and its soldiers were nearly depleted. As a result, he turned his attention west. He launched a foray into the

Western Roman Empire, ravaging and pillaging towns in modern-day Belgium and France, with the Byzantines now off his back. The savage Attila decimated the cities of Metz, Cambrai, Strasbourg, Rheims, Amiens, and Worms one after the other. A considerable number of former foes came together in what can only be described as a valiant last struggle to resist the supposedly unstoppable "Scourge of God." To resist this common menace, a sizable force of Romans under the command of the aforementioned Flavius Aetius united with their former adversaries, the Visigoths under King Theodoric I, as well as another barbarous tribe, the Alans under King Sangiban. Additionally, Attila and his Huns weren't alone. Formerly oppressed peoples such as the Ostrogoths, Gepids, Franks, Rugians, Sciri, Burgundians, and Thuringians joined them. At the town of Orlans, which the Huns had already started to assault and plunder, the two powerful forces first clashed. The Huns retreated east to a more advantageous place as the "allies" charged.

Although historians continue to disagree on the precise location of the fight, almost all agree that it took place in eastern Champagne, between Troyes and Châlons. The area is referred to as the Catalaunian Plains (Campi Catalauni in Latin). Except for a hill that was the main landmark nearby, the terrain was essentially flat. To gain the upper ground and advance first, both forces rushed to the location. The Hunnic attack was successfully repelled by the Romans and Visigoths, who also took control of it. Both sides suffered significant casualties, and when the Visigoth heavy cavalry saw an opening, they stormed down the hill, overwhelming the Huns and forcing them back.

Attila withdrew after realizing he had lost the battle. By the time the fight was over, the Visigoth King had been killed, and the blood had flowed like a river down the hill. But thanks to the Romans' and their allies' success, Western Europe was protected from the vicious Huns. Attila launched another offensive a year later, in 452 AD, but this time he was seeking retribution. He had the Italian Peninsula in mind. He and his soldiers crossed the Alps and started pillaging the northern Italian cities of Aquileia, Padua, Verona, and Mediolanum (Milan). According to mythology, only His Holiness Pope Leo I (the Great) succeeded in convincing the "Scourge of God" to spare Rome and return home.

The more likely scenario is that the Huns decided to return home on their initiative because they were loaded down with loot and the region was being plagued at the time. Whatever the case, Attila would pass away from a severe nose bleed a year later after passing out drunk on his wedding night. His mighty and terrible kingdom would collapse as a result of numerous internal power struggles, and after his passing, the Huns vanished from Europe just as quickly as they had appeared a century earlier.

Conclusion

Greetings on finishing this book! Although I'm sure you have a lot under your belt already, don't forget to give Amazon a genuine review. If you found this information useful, please spread the word to anyone else you believe would find these topics interesting.

CPSIA information can be obtained
at www.ICGtesting.com
Printed in the USA
BVHW050544140223
658474BV00023B/362

9 783986 539627